www.wadsworth.com

wadsworth.com is the World Wide Web site
for Wadsworth and is your direct
source to dozens of online resources.

At *wadsworth.com* you can find out about
supplements, demonstration software, and
student resources. You can also send email to
many of our authors and preview new publications
and exciting new technologies.

wadsworth.com
Changing the way the world learns®

Assessment for Crisis Intervention

A TRIAGE ASSESSMENT MODEL

RICK A. MYER
Duquesne University

BROOKS/COLE

THOMSON LEARNING

Australia • Canada • Mexico • Singapore • Spain
United Kingdom • United States

BROOKS/COLE

THOMSON LEARNING

Counseling Editor: Julie Martinez
Editorial Assistant: Marin Plank
Marketing Manager: Caroline Concilla
Signing Representative: Kelly McKeever
Project Editor: Matthew Stevens
Print Buyer: Tandra Jorgensen
Permissions Editor: Joohee Lee

Production Service: G&S Typesetters, Inc.
Text Designer: Janet Wood
Copy Editor: Sue Carter
Cover Designer: Yvo Riezebos
Cover Printer: Webcom Limited
Compositor: G&S Typesetters, Inc.
Printer: Webcom Limited

Wadsworth/Thomson Learning
10 Davis Drive
Belmont, CA 94002-3098
USA

For more information about our products, contact us:
**Thomson Learning Academic Resource Center
1-800-423-0563**
http://www.wadsworth.com

International Headquarters
Thomson Learning
International Division
290 Harbor Drive, 2nd Floor
Stamford, CT 06902-7477
USA

UK/Europe/Middle East/South Africa
Thomson Learning
Berkshire House
168-173 High Holborn
London WC1V 7AA
United Kingdom

Asia
Thomson Learning
60 Albert Street, #15-01
Albert Complex
Singapore 189969

Canada
Nelson Thomson Learning
1120 Birchmount Road
Toronto, Ontario M1K 5G4
Canada

Library of Congress Cataloging-in-Publication Data
Myer, Rick.
Assessment for crisis intervention : a triage assessment model / Rick A. Myer.
p. cm.
Includes index.
ISBN 0-534-36232-X
1. Crisis intervention (Mental health services)   I. Title.

RC480.6 .M925 2000
362.2′04251—dc21

00-044468

This book is printed on acid-free recycled paper.

Table of Contents

Chapter 6

Using the Triage Assessment Form: Crisis Intervention 109

Appendix A:

Ethical and Legal Issues 141

Appendix B:

Triage Assessment Form: Crisis Intervention 147

Index 151

List of Tables

List of Figures

Preface

When clients come to you in crisis, how do you know what to do? What are you looking for? What sort of assessment process do you use as you listen to clients tell their story? Do you follow a model for or have you mapped out what is important as you listen? Or do you simply go with the flow, letting clients say whatever they would like? In addition, how do you know if you are addressing the most important issues related to the crisis? How do you make decisions as to which techniques, strategies, and skills are needed to help clients? This book is written to answer those questions.

Unfortunately, the assessment process is often overlooked in the crisis intervention literature. At most, authors devote a chapter to the topic, and often just a portion of a chapter. Yet, I believe assessment is the most critical aspect of crisis intervention because it guides the intervention and tells you what you need to know to help your clients. Without accurate assessment, you are left to fumble around using trial and error until you find an effective method of helping clients. We all have a model by which we assess clients, but it is often implicit and sometimes not very efficient. This book can help you organize your thoughts and design a model that will help you obtain the information needed to help clients in crisis.

The book is intended for anyone who is asked to help people in crisis, including (a) professionals such as psychologists, social workers, school counselors, ministers, community counselors, and marriage and family therapists; (b) volunteer crisis workers who work on hotlines or in domestic violence centers, sexual assault centers, and other agencies that provide services to people in crisis; and (c) frontline helpers such as police officers and firefighters.

The goal is for readers to develop a model for the assessment process in crisis intervention. The triage assessment model, which focuses on affective, cognitive, and behavioral reactions, can provide you with a basic framework. The Triage Assessment Form: Crisis Intervention (TAF) operationalizes the triage assessment model and can guide you in devising efficient and effective interventions. You can try out the triage assessment model and the TAF to determine how they fit your situation and the type of clients you see, adjusting it to suit your particular needs.

This book can also be useful to students as a basis for understanding people's reactions to crisis situations. Too often, training programs leave students to sink or swim when it comes to helping clients in crisis, trusting that they will learn the necessary skills in practica and at internship sites. This oversight is a grievous error: The one type of client all professionals encounter are those in crisis. We can avoid working with families, we can refer problems that involve sexual issues to others, we can choose not to see clients with addictions, and we can specify the age group we work with; but we cannot escape seeing clients in crisis.

Instructors and trainers can use the book as supplemental material for courses in which crisis intervention and/or assessment is taught. As a supplement to other material, this book can help instructors teach students the basic skills needed to understand clients in crisis. Practical examples are used that ground the principles discussed in each chapter in real-life situations. These examples can be used for role plays or as discussion starters. Study questions that facilitate further in-depth discussions are also provided for each chapter.

Trainers conducting workshops for paraprofessionals will also find many uses for this book. The book is based on research, but is accessible and offers many practical suggestions for how to assess someone who is in crisis.

During the past 10 to 15 years, the field of crisis intervention has been increasingly recognized as a speciality area. With the recent upsurge in violent acts in schools, churches, and communities, the need has never been so great for people trained to help those in crisis. The focus of this book, the assessment process, is an important aspect of that training. Chapter 1 provides an overview of crisis intervention assessment, defining crucial terms and explaining the role of assessment, as well as differentiating assessment for crisis intervention from other types of assessment. After describing the benefits and drawbacks of different models of crisis assessment, Chapter 2 introduces the triage assessment model, which, as noted, covers the areas of affective, cognitive, and behavioral reactions to crisis. The next three chapters zero in on the individual dimensions of the model; Chapter 3 addresses affective reactions, Chapter 4 discusses cognitive reactions, and Chapter 5 focuses on behavioral reactions. Each chapter outlines the crisis worker's role, provides a research-based rationale for using each component in that dimension, and describes how to assess clients' reactions as well as the severity of those reactions. Finally, Chapter 6 focuses on application of the model using the TAF. This chapter also includes three case studies to demonstrate the use of the TAF with clients. And, although this chapter mentions treatment, that is not the focus of this book. Information on integrating the TAF and treatment can be found in *Crisis Intervention Strategies* by James and Gilliland. These authors briefly discuss the TAF and then integrate it throughout their discussion of specific types of crises.

Finally, I want to thank the reviewers for their constructive comments, which helped to sharpen my focus as I worked on the book. I also want to thank the Duquesne University doctoral students who helped by offering suggestions and proofing sections of the book. A special thanks to Sarah, my wife, who also provided editorial help as I completed the book. Without her, I would probably still be writing.

INTRODUCTION TO CRISIS ASSESSMENT

The field of crisis intervention has blossomed since the 1970s (Aguilera, 1994; Hoff, 1995). This growth has not been limited to professional human service workers or the agencies they work for (Hendricks & McKean, 1995); many people and organizations have become involved in offering crisis intervention services. Churches, community groups, business clubs, and so forth, have joined in an effort to assist people who for whatever reason are struggling with problems and issues that overwhelm their ability to cope or access available resources. This grass-roots type of development has led to the creation of a large number of programs. Some of these endeavors are time limited, such as helping people rebuild their lives after a flood. Other programs are ongoing in their efforts to help people experiencing a specific type of crisis such as medical problems, teen pregnancy, rape, or addictive behaviors. The common element, whether a person is a trained professional or a volunteer, is that he or she cares and wants to help.

Yet, a desire to help, while commendable, is not enough. Crisis workers need to be trained (Hendricks & McKean, 1995). Unfortunately, most professionals learn crisis intervention through on-the-job training. That is, they learn the needed skills through a trial-and-error method while helping a client through a crisis situation. Professionals soon learn that basic therapeutic skills, while useful, are not sufficient in crisis situations. They realize that the ability to think quickly and creatively is critical in order to provide services. Within this process, professionals discover they need to develop efficient and effective assessment skills. Surprisingly, volunteers may receive more specific training for crisis intervention than professionals. Generally, volunteers must sit through extensive training sessions to learn the needed skills. Much of this training involves learning basic helping skills for use in crisis situations. The volunteers also learn the boundaries within which they work due to their restricted training. Generally the training such volunteers receive enables them to be effective as professionals doing crisis intervention.

A key but sometimes overlooked element in effective crisis intervention is assessment (Myer, Williams, Ottens, & Schmidt, 1992). Assessment should be ongoing, monitoring clients' reactions to determine what level of intervention is needed. Does a client need to be hospitalized? Is the client contemplating committing suicide or harming someone else? What resources are needed for this client to resolve the crisis situation? What approach will be the most effective for the client at this time? These questions and many more are constantly being weighed by crisis workers. Answers are found in the crisis workers' ability to apply reliable assessment procedures over a wide range of situations. This book describes a holistic assessment process that can be applied to crisis situations. The model provides crisis workers with a structure and format for assessment that, when used properly, helps in the treatment of people in crisis. First, however, a basic introduction to crisis intervention is needed.

GROWTH OF CRISIS INTERVENTION

I believe the interest in crisis intervention is an outgrowth of three interrelated phenomena. First, all people experience a crisis sometime in their lives. Tragedy strikes everyone regardless of ethnicity, socioeconomic status, or gender; no one can insulate him- or herself from crises. Roberts (1996) reported that 130 million situational crisis events are experienced each year in the United States. No one can predict whether or not he or she will fall victim to a violent crime or experience some other random event such as a car accident. Other crises may involve the discovery of a terminal illness or job loss. Rabbi Kushner (1981) said it well with his phrase, "When bad things happen to good people." Some crises may be specific to a culture, yet many others are universal. For example, being a victim of violent crime is a universal crisis. However, teen pregnancy is a situation which one culture views as a crisis but which another culture views as commonplace. In any case, no one is immune from unforeseen crisis events, and the number of such events seems to have increased. Crisis workers can provide the short-term assistance people need as they cope with the aftermath of a crisis. This assistance should lead people toward developing or mobilizing the resources needed to restore them to their previous level of functioning (James & Gilliland, 2001).

Second, two somewhat indirect but distinct social phenomena have led to increasing numbers of people seeking professional help for psychological problems. For one thing, the geographic mobility of people in our society is such that many people do not live close to their extended family. In the past, people in crisis would turn to family for support. Now, they are more likely to turn to people such as crisis workers because family members are not close by. A second factor influencing the increase in people seeking professional help is the high incidence of violence in our society (Hendricks & McKean, 1995). Whereas once we might have believed ourselves safe from the most violent of crimes, we no longer have that assurance. Gangs, drugs, and other perils have made their way even into the once safer rural areas. Violent acts are occurring with such frequency and indiscriminateness that no one can consider him- or herself insulated from these acts. At times, such crises are even experienced vicariously (Dingman & Ginter, 1995). For example, someone may fall victim to a drive-by shooting, and although a person in another city is not directly affected, he or she may experience a crisis, afraid of becoming a victim to a similar situation.

A third reason for this growth is that professionals are recognizing that unless people satisfactorily resolve their reaction to a crisis situation, they may develop more invasive psychological problems (James & Gilliland, 2001; Hobbs, 1984). Schwartz (1997) believes that traumas have a neurological impact that can result in physiological changes in the brain. If untreated, such individuals may later experience any of a wide range of diagnosable mental illnesses (e.g., eating disorders or post-traumatic stress disorder). Schwartz adds that in some instances borderline personality disorder or a dissociative disorder may result. Thus the resolution of affective, cognitive, and behavioral reactions that occur as a result of a crisis is in a sense a type of mental illness prevention.

DEFINING CRISIS

The first step in cultivating the skills needed to help people in crisis is to construct a definition of crisis. Using James and Gilliland (2001) as a basis, crisis can be defined as follows: Crisis is a perception of an event or situation as an intolerable difficulty that exceeds the person's *immediately available* resources and coping mechanisms. This definition can be divided into four components:

> *"Crisis is a perception"*—The crisis must be viewed from the client's perspective, not the crisis worker's. An event that seems trivial to a crisis worker can be a major crisis for a client. A client's perception generally involves both realistic and distorted interpretations of the crisis event.
> *"of an event or situation"*—A crisis is the reaction to a specific event or situation. This event or situation usually can be readily identified by clients. Certain events or situations are universally considered a crisis (e.g., victimization of violent crimes, suffering through a natural disaster), while others are more culturally variable (e.g., teenage pregnancy, moving away from home). On occasion clients may have difficulty pinpointing the crisis event. This situation usually occurs when clients postpone seeking treatment and/or have not satisfactorily resolved a previous traumatic event.

"as an intolerable difficulty"—A crisis event must be understood by clients as unbearable. They must believe the event to be overwhelming and perplexing. This may mean that the problem is too complex for them to sort out or that they lack the necessary knowledge or skills to cope with the situation.

"that exceeds the person's immediately available *resources and coping mechanisms."*—Clients must believe they do not have the resources immediately available to prevail over the situation. I emphasize the phrase *immediately available:* A person might have had the resources to cope a month ago, but today he or she does not.

It is important at this point to differentiate between developmental and situational crises. The reaction to these types of crisis can be similar, but the dynamics are different.

Developmental Crises

Developmental crises can be described as events that are commonly experienced in growth and maturation (Aguilera, 1994). As people move through various stages (e.g., marriage, childbirth, children leaving home, retirement, death of a loved one) in their lives, they may experience crises as they adapt to these situations. The more important the event, the more potential there is for a crisis reaction. Also, the more the event corresponds to culturally accepted patterns and timetables, the less likely a crisis reaction. For example, in Western cultures children are expected to move away from home and become independent when they reach adulthood. However, in other cultures, it is more acceptable to stay in the home, and children are not expected to become independent. Therefore, if a child remains in the home and dependent upon parents in the United States, a crisis may develop for the parents. In another culture, the parents might experience a crisis if their adult child *leaves* home. Another example is cultural norms about pregnancy. If a woman is expected to become pregnant in her teens and she does not, a crisis situation may develop. In the United States, by contrast, teen pregnancy may precipitate a crisis.

Situational Crises

Situational crises are those events that occur unexpectedly during the course of a person's life. Such crises are usually sudden and/or cannot be controlled. These include both natural disasters (e.g., floods, earthquakes, hurricanes) and human-caused disasters (e.g., acts of violence, car accidents, job loss). Reactions to the two types of situational crises are likely to differ (Ofman, Mastria, & Steinberg, 1995). If the crisis was precipitated by human action, people may ask whether the act was premeditated and intentional, or accidental. For natural disasters, questions tend to be framed in terms of time; people wonder when the disaster will be over so recovery can begin. Generally, situational crises transcend cultural differences. In most cultures, acts of violence are considered a crisis. For example, rape is rape no matter the culture; murder is murder no matter the culture. Similarly, natural disasters result in crisis situations regardless of culture. The destruction of property, disruption of daily activities, and loss of life resulting from natural disasters always cause various levels of trauma for the people involved.

A basic knowledge of crisis events is the first step for crisis workers in developing the skills needed to help people in crisis. This understanding provides crisis workers with the building blocks to begin constructing a working definition of crisis intervention.

DEFINING CRISIS INTERVENTION

Crisis intervention is time-limited treatment directed at reactions to a specific event in order to help the client return to a precrisis level of functioning. This definition involves three distinct elements that, when combined, provide crisis workers with a structure for helping people. This structure guides the intervention process, helping crisis workers understand the parameters, reasons, and goal for this type of therapy.

Time-Limited Dimension

First, crisis intervention is time limited (Hendricks & McKean, 1995), with a duration of not more than 6 weeks. During this time, the crisis worker may meet with a person once or many times. Because of the uniqueness of each situation, crisis workers must be creative in scheduling appointments that may be as short as a few minutes or stretch to several hours. A general guideline in scheduling appointments is to *stay with or schedule appointments with a person long enough to ensure physical and psychological safety.* This means that crisis workers may spend several hours with a person who is suicidal and/or homicidal in order to hospitalize or talk the person out of doing harm to self or others. Crisis workers may also need to schedule short (15- to 30-minute) appointments several times each week until the person has stabilized. Crisis workers should be concerned not only about physical safety but also about psychological well-being. They should also be alert for situations in which a person is vulnerable to manipulation of others and not capable of self-care. Meetings should be tailored to help the person regain a sense of psychological equilibrium and self-protection.

The time-limited nature of crisis intervention means that crisis workers should take an action-oriented approach in order to help clients resolve the issue (James & Gilliland, 2001). In general, *the more severe the reaction to the crisis situation, the more active the crisis worker must be.* Crisis workers, however, must guard against letting clients become too dependent. If the reaction is severe enough to warrant some dependence, the crisis worker should wean the client away from this dependence as soon as possible.

Single-Issue Dimension

Second, treatment addresses a specific issue and attempts to help clients resolve only that concern (Cournoyer, 1996). The crisis intervention process *must therefore be focused on setting and maintaining realistic goals.* These goals are necessarily limited in scope; only symptoms related to the crisis situation are relevant. Crisis workers must constantly discipline themselves to focus on immediate needs and not become side-tracked. If other issues are identified, these should be discussed at the conclusion of the crisis intervention, at which point crisis workers can either switch to a more traditional therapeutic approach or refer clients to someone experienced with that issue.

The outcome of crisis intervention is not major personality changes. Expecting major transformations only leads to frustration for crisis workers. While some people may make drastic life changes resulting from crisis experiences, more often they do not. Crisis workers must be satisfied with helping a person successfully navigate a specific situation. For most situations, in fact, crisis workers should caution clients not to make impulsive changes, which are often part of the person's attempt to solve the crisis.

Treatment Dimension

Third, treatment focuses on clients returning to a precrisis level of functioning (James & Gilliland, 2001). When crises occur, coping skills may improve, remain the same, or deteriorate. One factor that helps determine the outcome is the intervention process. Slaikeu (1990) distinguishes between two levels of crisis intervention. First-order intervention, or "psychological first-aid," is usually given on site by whoever is the first on the scene. Police, emergency medical personnel, and firefighters are included in this group. Often, this is the only contact these people have with the person in crisis. *The goal of first-order intervention is to reestablish immediate coping and provide support.* The focus is on the present, the here-and-now, not on long-term issues or long-standing problems. Crisis workers must use their energy and funnel clients' energies on what must be done immediately to begin the process of resolving the crisis. In addition, first-order intervention will help people find resources they need for more extended treatment or the resources needed to assist them during the crisis. This type of intervention leads to the maintenance of coping skills by helping clients direct their efforts in a productive way.

The goal of second-order intervention, or "crisis therapy," is the *integration of the experience into clients' lives by developing new coping skills, adapting to the crisis, or both* (Slaikeu, 1990). This type of intervention is usually conducted by professionals in the human services field—social workers, psychologists, counselors, marriage and family therapists, or psychiatric nurses, to name a few. In this phase of crisis intervention, crisis workers will generally have several contacts with people in crisis to help them resolve the crisis. These crisis workers need training in personality, abnormal psychology, and therapeutic strategies and approaches to helping others. Intervention at this level also involves anticipatory guidance (Aguilera, 1994). Crisis workers must be knowledgeable and able to advise people in crisis about the experience. For example, crisis workers in domestic violence centers should be able to inform women who enter the facility about how to obtain orders of protection. Crisis workers in hospital emergency rooms should know hospital policies and procedures when a person is brought to the emergency room (Myer & Hanna, 1996). Many people are not familiar with hospital routine and need guidance during this time.

CRISIS ASSESSMENT ISSUES

Effective crisis intervention depends on quick and accurate assessment (Hoff, 1995). Crisis workers must quickly—often within minutes—evaluate clients' reactions and initiate treatment; therefore the need for reliable assessment procedures are crucial. Understanding the importance of the assessment process as well as recognizing how crisis assessment differs from other assessment procedures can increase crisis workers' effectiveness.

Importance of Assessment

Failure to correctly assess crisis reactions can be hazardous to both the person in crisis and the crisis worker (Hoff, 1995). Faulty assessment leads to ineffective helping and may lead to the development of destructive psychological disturbances in the person experiencing the crisis (James & Gilliland, 2001). Poor assessment techniques may result from inattention in one or more areas on the part of the crisis worker. First, crisis workers may fail to be attentive. They may be thinking of another client, a program they are planning, what they are going to do after work, and so on. A failure to give attention or listen to clients always leads to inadequate assessment. Second, crisis workers might be thinking that they have heard this problem hundreds of times and therefore a set treatment is needed. Crisis workers must remember that each person reacts differently, and therefore treatment needs will differ, even if they have worked with many people with similar crises. Failure to provide individual service can be considered negligence and therefore unethical. (See Appendix A for a summary of ethical and legal issues related to crisis intervention.) Inattention may result in treatment that is either ineffective or possibly harmful to the person in crisis. Third, crisis workers may not be aware of their limitations, believing that they should be able to help everyone regardless of the problem. This belief can lead to burnout (James & Gilliland, 2001). Crisis workers must be willing to admit that they cannot be responsible for the actions of their clients. This issue is particularly acute when a person in crisis commits suicide in spite of crisis workers' best efforts to stop this act. Crisis workers should not assume they will be perfect and be able to help everyone. Supervision is one method of helping crisis workers come to accept this assertion. Crisis workers must always be aware of the need for supervision and consultation, particularly when working with a person who is suicidal and/or homicidal. Care must be taken to document times and content of meetings to provide evidence that crisis workers were acting within the due standard of care for that type of crisis (Bednar, Bednar, Lambert, & Waite, 1991). Fourth, inadequate training can also lead to poor assessment techniques. Crisis workers must have training in crisis theory and assessment if they are to be efficient and effective with their interventions.

Effects of Overhospitalization   One outcome of poor assessment is overhospitalization (Hoff, 1995). Rather than help a person learn new coping skills and address the crisis situation, some crisis workers may opt to diagnose people in order to have them admitted to a hospital. Hoff believes this is an injustice to both the person and the mental health system. *A basic assumption in crisis intervention is that most reactions in crises are not pathological* (Shapiro & Koocher, 1996). While reactions may be acute, impairing day-to-day functioning of a person, they do not necessarily indicate the need for hospitalization. To simply diagnose a person who is reacting to a crisis situation amounts to seeing a crisis reaction as an illness rather than an opportunity for growth (Hoff, 1995). Viewing crisis reactions as an illness may depersonalize treatment; but people in crisis need support, not treatment that is dispensed in a routine, impersonal manner. Crisis workers must be cautious when choosing to diagnose a person and recommending hospitalization. At times, hospitalization is warranted, but not often. While all crisis workers should seek consultation prior to diagnosing a person in crisis and recommending hospitalization, beginning crisis workers may require more assistance. If in doubt, always seek a second, and even third, opinion prior to labeling a person with a diagnosis and recommending hospitalization. This process will help ensure the best care for people in crisis and protect crisis workers from engaging in negligent treatment practices.

Effects of Erroneous Assessment   The effects of erroneous assessment can be serious. Hoff (1995) states that using a crisis approach when there is only the appearance of a crisis is ill advised. Responding excessively may result in people believing the only way to receive services is to convince crisis workers that they are in crisis. According to Hoff, this may lead to people to use suicidal behaviors as the way to obtain help. Assessment, therefore, should be conducted with care in order to determine the nature of the crisis and reactions to the situation.

There are three ways in which crisis workers can detect people who appear to be in crisis when in fact they are not. *First, crisis workers should be alert for contradictory reactions.* Experience is essential to discerning inconsistent re-actions since, when in crisis, people tend to behave erratically. Being watchful for seeming incompatibility in the intensity of reactions is one way to assess if a crisis is occurring. *Second, crisis workers should be aware of symptoms of mental illness and malingering.* Such awareness helps prevent abuse of the sys-tem. However, many crisis workers are not professional mental health workers; I encourage these volunteers to seek consultation when people disclose "crazy" sounding problems or something the crisis worker has never heard before. *Third, a healthy dose of skepticism is needed for the assessment process in cri-sis situations.* Crisis workers must assess the meaning and intent of people's re-actions in crisis situations, continually asking questions of themselves and clients in order to ensure that they understand what they are being told. This healthy skepticism helps avert reinforcing crisis behavior and misuse of the mental health system.

Holistic Considerations   Crisis workers too often fail to assess the whole person, frequently focusing on clients' emotional reactions. This can result in premature termination from treatment. Once people have become calm, it is believed, the crisis is over. Crisis workers also need to asses cognitive and be-havioral reactions, however. Failure to assess these areas means they are not treated and may result in the development of other psychological problems that may reveal themselves months to years later in the person's life. Research on traumatic experiences indicates that unresolved crises manifest themselves in more damaging psychological problems (Schwartz, 1997). Crisis workers must consider the whole person in the assessment process in order to prevent premature termination from treatment.

Differentiation of Assessment Methods

Within the mental health field several different types of assessment approaches may be used. Four of the most commonly used are diagnostic assessment, stan-dardized testing assessment, symptom assessment, and psychosocial history as-sessment. These approaches use specific techniques and are generally associ-ated with different disciplines—psychiatry, psychology, and social work. Each strategy has benefits and drawbacks and can be valuable for learning about and describing clients. However, for crisis intervention, these approaches may have limited usefulness. Table 1.1 compares these approaches with assessment for crisis intervention. This comparison underscores the differences of these

TABLE 1.1

APPROACHES TO ASSESSMENT

	Diagnostic Assessment	Standardized Testing Assessment	Symptom Assessment	Psycho/Social History Assessment	Crisis Assessment
Goal/Outcome	Categorize/Label (Hohenshil, 1996)	Develops profile of client that identifies weaknesses and/or strengths. Used for placement, selection, or prediction purposes (Friedenberg, 1995; Walsh & Betz, 1995)	Identifies symptoms that may require further assessment and/or treatment. Used to screen clients (Spielberger, et al., 1995)	Describe developmental, psychological, and social history of clients for treatment planning and case management (Morrison, 1995; Hepworth & Larson, 1993; Connaway & Gentry, 1988)	Gather information regarding crisis situation in order to assist client in mobilizing resources as quickly as possible (James & Gilliland, 2001; Hoff, 1989)
Process	Fixed process using interviews and/or standardized tests, both objective and projective. However, as symptoms alter, diagnosis may be changed (Kellerman & Berry, 1997)	Fixed process using standardized tests as focus of assessment. May use objective, projective, or a combination of both (Acklin, 1995)	Fixed process using symptom inventories or checklists that are most often self-report (Groth-Marnat, 1990; Spielberger, et al., 1995)	Fixed process using interviews and survey forms (Morrison, 1995; Hepworth & Larson, 1993)	Ongoing throughout crisis intervention using interviews (Greenstone & Leviton, 1993; Hendricks & McKean, 1995)
Relationship to Treatment	Indirect, labels client in order to develop treatment (Kellerman & Berry; Hohenshil, 1996)	Indirect, profile assists in developing treatment plans (Kellerman & Berry, 1997; Beutler & Harwood, 1995; Hanyes, 1995)	Indirect, may be used to guide standardized and/or diagnostic assessment. Also may be used to guide referral process (Beutler & Harwood, 1995)	Indirect, used to determine historical/environmental context of client problem to help develop treatment plan and case management issues (Wood & Robinson, 1996; Hepworth & Larson, 1993)	Direct, information gathered used to help client re-establish sense of equilibrium (James & Gilliland, 2001; Aguilera, 1994)

	Materials Needed	Time Involved	Information Gathered	Training	What is Assessed
	Interview schedules, mental status exam, and standardized tests (Kellerman & Berry, 1997; Herson & Turner, 1987)	15 minutes to 1½ hours	Catalogs symptoms in order to determine diagnostic label (Kellerman & Berry, 1997)	Licensed Professional Usually Ph.D. or M.D.	Symptoms that are used to infer presence of disease (Walsh & Berry, 1995)
	Tests, manuals, scoring sheets and facilities to administer tests. Also may need access to computer to score some tests	15 minutes to 2 hours	Varies depending on tests. May be about specific area or general personality characteristics. Sample of behavior under controlled conditions (Walsh & Betz, 1995)	Varies on level of test. Always requires a course in testing. Intelligence tests and projectives require special training (Finkelstien & Tuckman, 1997; Drummond, 1996)	Observations and self-report of behaviors, moods, and thinking
	Tests, manuals, scoring sheets and facilities to administer tests. Also may need access to computer to score some tests	5 to 20 minutes	Varies greatly depending on inventory or checklist. May be extremely narrow in focus or can be general in nature (Groth-Marnat, 1990)	Varies depending on inventory or checklist. Most often some type of formal training either in college or conference/seminar	Client's functioning on the symptoms included in the inventory or checklist
	Survey forms, interview schedules	30 minutes to 3 hours	Varies but includes demographic information, developmental history, family history, symptoms, current level of functioning, psychological history, and medical history (Woods & Robinson, 1996)	Bachelor's degree minimum with training. Master's degree generally preferred	Functioning of client from a psychological perspective within the environmental context (Woods & Robinson, 1996; Hepworth & Larson, 1993)
	Varies depending on situation. Most often interview schedules (James & Gilliland, 2001)	5 minutes, or until crisis is resolved.	Varies but includes safety information, nature of crisis situation, attempts to resolve, support systems (Hendricks & McKean, 1995)	No education level required. Training in crisis assessment needed	Clients current level of functioning (James & Gilliland, 2001; Hendricks & McKean, 1995; Slaikeu, 1990)

approaches as well as anchoring the concepts of crisis assessment in a broader assessment framework. In practice these approaches overlap to varying degrees.

Goal/Outcome   The goal among these assessment approaches differs. Except for symptom assessment and crisis assessment, each assessment approach attempts to be comprehensive in describing people; the goal is to characterize their nature. In contrast, symptom assessment evaluates clients along a band of symptoms ranging from narrow (e.g., the Beck Depression Inventory [BDI] [Beck & Steer, 1993]) to broad (e.g., the Symptom Check List 90-Revised [SCL 90-R] [Derogatis, 1994]). The goal of this type of assessment is generally to screen clients to determine if further assessment or treatment is warranted. Crisis assessment, on the other hand, assesses people's reaction to the immediate situation in order to mobilize the resources needed to resolve the problems associated with that situation. The goal of each approach is guided by the assumptions of the theory upon which it is built. The diagnostic assessment approach uses the medical model, which assumes that what is observed are symptoms of a disease. The label given to the disease is a shorthand way to describe a specific collection of symptoms. The standardized assessment approach is based on a psychological model. A basic supposition of this model is the concept of personality. Although a wide range of definitions exist for personality, it is generally believed that personality can be portrayed by describing various characteristics that are measured by self-report and/or observation. Similarly, symptom assessment builds on psychological research that identifies specific symptoms—affective, cognitive, and/or behavioral—as associated with psychological problems. A social work model is the basis for psychosocial history assessment approach. This approach assumes that to understand people, it is necessary to assess their history along with their interaction with the environment. Assessment must therefore be comprehensive, taking into account historical, environmental, social, and individual features. Crisis assessment is based on a crisis model. This model assumes that the crisis situation, with an emphasis on the client's perception of that situation, is the focal point for assessment.

Process   These five approaches to assessment utilize generally similar processes to gather information. Interviews—with clients, family members, and/or others, are typically an integral part of each approach. The interviews with others are used both to confirm the information provided by clients and to add to the information given by clients. In crisis assessment, in particular, clients' reactions may be so severe that they are unable to provide any information. For example, clients may be experiencing shock, blocking the situation from their awareness.

Standardized testing, symptom assessment, and psychosocial history assessment follow a somewhat different process. In addition to interviews, additional information is gathered in the assessment process. In standardized assessment, clients may be administered projective tests such as the Rorschach, the Thematic Apperception Test, or other similar tests. The information gathered during this portion of the process is added to the material collected from the interview. Symptom assessment utilizes self-report checklists or inventories to identify problem areas. Once identified, a determination is made to refer clients for further assessment or treatment. In addition to information from interviews, the psychosocial history approach also may use historical data; material from past records and family history information is an integral part and helps to generate the report that leads to treatment recommendations.

Relationship to Treatment   The goal of all assessment is to assist in the treatment of clients. However, the relationship of assessment to treatment varies, primarily with respect to when and how it is used. With diagnostic, personality, symptom, and psychosocial history assessments, information is gathered from clients for the purpose of writing a report, which typically includes recommendations for treatment. In these cases, there is a time lapse between gathering information and using it for treatment. In crisis intervention, information is gathered from clients and is used immediately. As clients exhibit their reactions to crisis situations, crisis workers must use this material to focus intervention strategies that will best help clients at that moment. Crisis workers do not have the luxury of being able to reflect on the information but instead must act quickly due to immediacy of the situation.

Materials Needed   The materials needed for each assessment approach are similar except for standardized testing assessment and symptoms assessment, which use testing manuals, scoring sheets, sheets to report results, and in some cases computer programs to score responses. The other three assessment approaches rely primarily on interviews. Although there is some variation in the material needed for the interview, such as surveys and schedules of questions, usually the bulk of the information is gathered through talking and asking questions. Other variations may occur and depend on the agency and/or person conducting the assessment.

Time Involved   The time needed for these approaches to assessment varies depending on experience, expertise, the materials being used, and, in crisis assessment, the immediate situation. As clinicians become seasoned they improve their ability to focus on the critical elements needed in the assessment. Expertise also influences the time needed, with the more expert clinicians requiring less time. Materials used also affect the time element. Typically, the more materials being used, the more time that is needed. Each of these variables will influence how long the assessment takes. In crisis assessment, however, the immediate situation is a primary determinant of the assessment process. Depending on the responsiveness of the client and the seriousness of the situation, the crisis worker may have to act immediately, using limited information. Clients may be too overcome with emotions to be able to talk coherently, or they may be nonresponsive altogether. In either situation, accurate information may be difficult to gather. Waiting until all the information is gathered may be impossible. If a person is assessed as suicidal, for example, clinicians must act accordingly, depending on the level of lethality, prior to having gathered all the information about the situation.

Information Gathered   The information collected during these assessment processes varies tremendously. Diagnostic assessment focuses on behaviors, cognitions, and feelings that suggest underlying problems that can be labeled. These labels are in a sense a shorthand for professionals to understand clients' problems. Standardized testing assessment gathers similar information, but the results are usually reported in the form of profiles and in psychological reports that summarize and integrate information from a number of tests. These tests may include personality, aptitude, intelligence, career, and achievement tests, to name a few. Tests may also vary from objective self-report instruments to projective tests that must be administered and interpreted by specially trained professionals. Information from symptom assessment is generally used to screen clients to ascertain if further testing or treatment is indicated. If additional testing is indicated, most often this process would involve the use of standardized tests. If treatment is needed, clients are referred to appropriate services and possibly for a diagnostic interview. Psychosocial history assessment gathers information from as many aspects of a person's life as possible. Material includes intrapersonal (internal) issues as well as extrapersonal (environmental) issues. Crisis assessment is much narrower in scope. The concern is compiling only the information that is needed to help a person mobilize the coping mechanisms and resources needed to overcome the situation causing the crisis.

Training   It is important for anyone conducting an assessment to be trained. However, different levels and types of training are needed depending on the nature of the assessment. Generally, more training is needed for the more technically complex assessment approaches, especially those that involve diagnosis. Diagnostic assessment requires an understanding of psychopathology. The standardized assessment approach also calls for a high level of training, including a knowledge of psychometrics and test construction. As with diagnostic assessment, the stakes are high because the person may be labeled as having a condition that could have serious consequences on his or her life. Specific training is also needed to conduct psychosocial history assessments. This system is also complex but has less of a potential for stamping a person in such a manner that would cause future difficulties, and thus less training is needed. Some training is needed to interpret results of symptom assessment. Generally, this training would involve a formal college-level course. However, in some instances training seminars conducted by various agencies may suffice. Of the five assessment approaches, crisis assessment requires the least training. This seems paradoxical since assessment in crisis intervention may involve life-and-death situations. However, the crisis worker does not need to understand subtle underlying issues that may be contributing to the concern being assessed. Diagnostic assessment, standardized testing, symptom assessment, and psychosocial history assessment require considerable knowledge of psychological development, abnormal psychology, and social/environmental factors that may influence behavior. This knowledge customarily comes through formal training leading to an advanced degree such as a master's or doctorate. With crisis assessment, training is needed, but not at the same level. It should provide a structure for understanding people's reactions to situations that overwhelm their coping abilities.

What Is Assessed   Each approach assesses clients from a different perspective in an attempt to collect information needed to help. The diagnostic approach assesses symptoms that are used to infer a disease. The disease cannot be observed directly, and therefore patterns of symptoms are used to label clients so that appropriate treatment plans can be made. Standardized testing assessment uses observations and self-report of behaviors, moods, and thinking in order to depict clients' strengths and weaknesses. In a sense, this is a snapshot or picture of clients that can be used to predict future behavior. Similarly, symptom assessment focuses on a limited segment of clients' lives. This information helps to guide the decision of whether or not clients need additional testing or treatment. The psychosocial history approach to assessment evaluates clients' functioning within society. This evaluation involves attempting to grasp the interactions of clients through understanding them as both being actors and being acted upon by the environment. Crisis assessment appraises clients' current level of functioning. Various models of crisis intervention assess different aspects of clients' reactions—behavioral, cognitive, affective—but all focus on the current level of functioning and issues related to the immediate situation.

Again, in practice these approaches to assessment overlap. There are few if any pure applications; human problems tend to be too complex for that. For example, crisis workers would not stop a person from disclosing concerns that may not relate directly to crisis situation. That material may help crisis workers understand a person more fully and be used to recommend treatment after the crisis has been resolved. Similar examples can be given for each approach. I have attempted to differentiate among the five to help crisis workers see how crisis assessment fits into the larger assessment picture.

SUMMARY

Crisis intervention is a growing human services field, and providing useful crisis intervention services depends on accurate assessment. Failure to correctly assess people's reactions leads to poor, inadequate services. An understanding of the other types of assessment, and how crisis assessment is similar to and different from them, can help crisis workers in their efforts to clearly articulate their own approach to assessment.

POINTS TO REMEMBER

- The growth of crisis intervention can be attributed to four factors: (1) All people experience crises; (2) people increasingly live far away from extended family; (3) violence has increased; and (4) research and experience indicate that inadequate resolution of crisis can result in mental illness.
- A crisis is a perception of an event or situation as an intolerable difficulty that exceeds a person's immediately available resources and coping mechanisms.
- Developmental crises are events commonly experienced in growth and maturation.
- Situational crises are events that occur unexpectedly during a person's life.
- Crisis intervention involves time-limited treatment focusing on a single issue with the goal of returning a person to precrisis level of functioning.
- A basic assumption is that most reactions in crises are not pathological.
- Crisis workers must be alert for contradictory symptoms, evidence of mental illness, and malingering, and they must maintain a sense of skepticism when assessing crisis reactions to ensure accurate assessments.
- Five basic assessment approaches in mental health are diagnostic, standardized testing, symptom, psychosocial history, and crisis assessment.
- Crisis assessment can be differentiated from other types of assessment approaches by considering the goal/outcome of assessment, the process used to conduct the assessment, the relationship of treatment to assessment, materials needed and time involved in the assessment, the information gathered during the assessment, training needed to conduct the assessment, and what is assessed.

STUDY QUESTIONS

1. How do situational and developmental crises differ? How are these alike? Are there any differences in how crisis workers would provide services to a person experiencing these crises?
2. Name a few of the possible outcomes of poor assessment in crisis situations. How would you avoid these?
3. Of the five approaches to assessment described in this chapter (diagnostic, standardized testing, psychosocial, crisis), which is the most similar and most different to crisis assessment?

REFERENCES

Acklin, M. W. (1995). How to select personality tests: A brief historical view. In J. E. Butcher (Ed.), *Clinical personality assessment: Practical approaches* (pp. 19–27). New York: Oxford University Press.

Aguilera, D. C. (1994). *Crisis intervention: Theory and methodology* (7th ed.). St. Louis: Mosby.

Anastasi, A., & Urbina, S. (1997). Psychological testing (7th ed.). Upper Saddle River, NJ: Prentice-Hall.

Beck, A. T., & Steer, R. A. (1993). *Beck Depression Inventory: Manual*. San Antonio, TX: Psychological Corporation.

Bednar, R. L., Bednar, S. C., Lambert, M. J., & Waite, D. R. (1991). *Psychotherapy with high-risk clients: Legal and professional standards*. Pacific Grove, CA: Brooks/Cole.

Beutler, L. E., & Harwood, T. M. (1995). How to assess clients in pretreatment planning. In J. E. Butcher (Ed.), *Clinical personality assessment: Practical approaches* (pp. 59–77). New York: Oxford University Press.

Cournoyer, B. R. (1996). Converging themes in crisis intervention, task-centered and brief treatment approaches. In A. R. Roberts (Ed.), *Crisis management and brief treatment* (pp. 3–15). Chicago: Nelson-Hall.

Derogatis, L. R. (1994). *SCL-90-R: Symptom Checklist 90-R: Administration, scoring, and procedures manual* (3rd ed.). Minneapolis, MN: National Computer Systems.

Dingman, R. L., & Ginter, E. J. (1995). Disasters and crises: The role of mental health counseling. *Journal of Mental Health Counseling, 17*, 259–263.

Drummond, R. J. (1996). *Appraisal procedures for counselors and helping professionals* (3rd ed.). Englewood Cliffs, NJ: Merrill.

Friedenberg, L. (1995). *Psychological testing: Design, analysis, and use*. Boston: Allyn & Bacon.

Greenstone, J. L., & Leviton, S. C. (1993). *Elements of Crisis Intervention: Crises and how to respond to them*. Pacific Grove, CA: Brooks/Cole.

Groth-Marnat, G. (1990). *Handbook of psychological assessment* (2nd ed.). New York: Wiley-Interscience.

Haynes, S. N. (1995). Introduction to the special section on chaos theory and psychological assessment. *Psychological Assessment, 7*, 3–4.

Hendricks, J. E., & McKean, J. B. (1995). *Crisis intervention: Contemporary issues for on-site interveners.* Springfield, IL: Thomas.

Hepworth, D. H., & Larsen, J. A. (1993). *Direct social work practice: Theory and skills* (4th ed.). Pacific Grove, CA: Brooks/Cole.

Hobbs, M. (1984). Crisis intervention in theory and practice: A selective review. *The British Psychological Society, 57,* 21–34.

Hoff, L. A. (1995). *People in crisis: Understanding and helping* (4th ed.). Redwood City, CA: Addison-Wesley.

Hohenshil, T. H. (1996). Editorial: Role of assessment and diagnosis in counseling. *Journal of Counseling and Development, 75,* 64–67.

James, R. K., & Gilliland, B. E. (2001). *Crisis intervention strategies* (4th ed.). Pacific Grove, CA: Brooks/Cole.

Kellerman, H., & Berry, A. (1997). *Handbook of psychodiagnostic testing: Analysis of personality in the psychological report* (3rd ed.). Boston: Allyn & Bacon.

Kushner, H. S. (1981). *When bad things happen to good people.* New York: Schocken.

Morrison, J. (1995). *The first interview: Revised for DSM-IV.* New York: Guilford.

Myer, R. A., & Hanna, F. J. (1996). Working in hospital emergency departments: Guidelines for crisis intervention workers. In A. R. Roberts (Ed.), *Crisis management and brief treatment* (pp. 37–59). Chicago: Nelson-Hall.

Myer, R. A., Williams, R. C., Ottens, A. J., & Schmidt, A. E. (1992). Crisis assessment: A three-dimensional model for triage. *Journal of Mental Health Counseling, 14,* 137–148.

Ofman, P. S., Mastria, M. A., & Steinberg, J. (1995). Mental health response to terrorism: The World Trade Center bombing. *Journal of Mental Health Counseling, 17,* 312–320.

Roberts, A. R. (1996). Epidemiology and definitions of acute crisis in American society. In A. R. Roberts (Ed.), *Crisis management and brief treatment* (pp. 16–34). Chicago: Nelson-Hall.

Schwartz, M. F. (1997, April). *Post traumatic stress disorder.* Keynote address at Crisis Convening XXI, Chicago.

Shapiro, D. E., & Koocher, G. P. (1996). Goals and practical considerations in outpatient medical crises intervention. *Professional Psychology: Research and Practice, 27,* 109–120.

Slaikeu, K. A. (1990). *Crisis intervention: A handbook for practice and research* (2nd ed.). Boston: Allyn & Bacon.

Spielberger, C. D., Ritterband, L. M., Sydeman, S. J., Reheiser, E. C., & Unger, K. K. (1995). Assessment of emotional states and personality traits: Measuring psychological vital signs. In J. E. Butcher (Ed.), *Clinical personality assessment: Practical approaches* (pp. 42–58). New York: Oxford University Press.

Turner, S. M., & Hersen, M. (1987). The interviewing process. In M. Hersen and S. M. Turner (Eds.), *Diagnostic interviewing* (3–24). New York: Plenum Press.

Walsh, W. B., & Betz, N. E. (1995). *Tests and assessment* (3rd ed.). Boston: Allyn & Bacon.

CRISIS ASSESSMENT MODELS

Amy is an attractive, 17-year-old senior in high school who will graduate in a few weeks. The crisis worker met her when she came to the sexual assault center after school. Amy said that she had been assaulted after attending a graduation party the past weekend. Initially Amy was quite controlled, but as she told her story she broke into tears. She said her parents had forbidden her to attend the party because they had suspicions it would be wild. Amy also admitted she knew the party would be wild and now she felt stupid, adding that if her parents found out, they would never let her leave home again. Through her weeping, Amy indicated that she had never done anything like this before and should have listened to her parents. Now she says that she believes it is too late and her dream of graduating and going away to college will never happen.

This brief vignette brings up many interesting and potentially confusing issues for crisis workers. Faced with situations similar to this, crisis workers must sift through information to understand the crisis and how to intervene in that situation. For Amy, what is the crisis situation? At first glance, the sexual assault would appear to be the crisis. However, with a closer reading at least two other issues stand out as possible crises: (a) disobeying her parents and (b) not being able to leave home to attend college. Another possibility is that the crisis is some combination of the three. Amy's cultural background also must be considered in order to assess her reaction. Not enough information is given in this vignette for an assessment, yet it does point out that crisis workers must be careful not to jump to conclusions. Instead, they must utilize their assessment skills to discern what information is important and what is not.

This chapter explores a variety of crisis assessment practices, examining the strengths and weaknesses of each, and then presents the triage assessment model, which will be the focus of the rest of the book. Read this chapter with a critical eye. Think about how each model can help you understand someone who is in crisis. More importantly, think about how you can adapt the triage assessment model to fit the way you do crisis intervention.

ASSESSMENT PRACTICES

Assessment practices are concerned with how information is gathered, and they vary from agency to agency. Often the specific method used by agencies is set by a governmental department or an organization providing grant money and serves ethical, legal, and/or clinical purposes. Such guidelines also function to promote accountability in ensuring agencies are operating within their mission. The three most common practices for crisis intervention are (a) conducting an interview; (b) administering standardized instruments designed to measure clients' responses to crisis-specific events; and (c) administering a standardized general personality instrument, the results of which are interpreted in light of the crisis. Each has value and provides worthwhile information, but each also can be ineffective if not used appropriately or if used by crisis workers who are not trained.

The interview appears to be the most widely used assessment practice in crisis intervention and falls on a continuum from unstructured to structured. The unstructured interview is a "shotgun" approach to assessment, with crisis workers posing questions in a seemingly random manner. However, when a specific crisis such as suicidal ideations are suspected, questions may be posed using predetermined content (Booner, 1990). By asking questions in a scattered manner, crisis workers hope to uncover material that will lead to effective intervention. Questions used in this approach usually fall within crisis workers' previous experience and assumptions about what is needed to help people. If a crisis worker typically employs a cognitive approach, the questions asked will center on perception. If crisis workers are more affective oriented, they will be inclined to ask questions designed to assess emotions. The benefit of the unstructured interview is its flexibility. Because crisis workers are not tied to a specific set of questions or protocol, they are able to respond as information emerges during the interview process. This method promotes rapport building and facilitates probing into important information. However, the unstructured interview also can overwhelm crisis workers with incoherent and disjointed pieces of information. When this situation takes place, crisis workers may fail to assess important aspects of clients' reactions. This issue is particularly relevant when crisis workers assess a client from a culture different from their own. Differences in language, speed, tempo of daily life, and urban and rural subcultures all impact the assessment process (Hinkle, 1994).

Structured interviews have the same risk, but for a different reason. Structured interviews typically involve asking a set of predetermined questions (Durlak & Roth, 1983). Crisis workers may become so intent on getting through the list that they fail to fully explore some areas and miss others because they simply are not on the list. The list of questions may also be culturally biased, assuming clients will understand all the questions, by not including culturally relevant questions. Structure can also make establishment of rapport difficult. If crisis workers become too intent on asking all the questions instead of listening to clients, clients may feel they have been treated poorly. The advantage of this method, however, is that crisis workers are less likely to forget to ask questions. This results in a higher probability of gathering information that will be useful for treatment planning. Also, structured interviews are not at the whim of crisis workers' theoretical predisposition, thereby increasing the likelihood of greater balance of gathered information.

Another common practice in crisis assessment is the use of instruments developed to measure clients' reactions to specific crisis events. These instruments are published on most conceivable crisis situations for all age groups. Because of the severity and complexity of suicide, many instruments measuring suicidal ideations have been published. A quick glance at catalogs of testing publishers confirms this belief. The Psychological Assessment Resources (2000) winter catalog lists two instruments, the Suicidal Behavior History Form and the Suicidal Ideation Questionnaire, while the Psychological Corporation (2000) lists the Beck Scale for Suicidal Ideation. Other examples of these types of instruments are the Veronen-Kilpatrick Modified Fear Survey (Resnick, Veronen, Kilpatrick, Calhoun, & Atkeson, 1986), for victims of sexual assault; the Jackson Incest Blame Scale (Jackson & Ferguson, 1983), for clients who have experienced incest; the Pediatric Emotional Distress Scale (Saylor, Swenson, Reynolds, & Taylor, 1999) and the Childhood Trauma Questionnaire (Bernstein & Fink, 1997), for children who have experienced a traumatic event; and the Mississippi Scale–Hostage Version (Keane, Caddell, & Taylor, 1988), for clients who have been victims of hostage takers. The benefit of these instruments is that they provide information applicable to a specific crisis event, as well as the means of monitoring these clients during treatment. By providing valuable information regarding the number and severity of symptoms associated with a specific crisis, such instruments can help crisis workers plan treatment on an individual basis. These instruments may also permit crisis workers to predict the course of treatment and the symptoms that will emerge as treatment progresses. Such instruments have serious drawbacks, however. Symptoms not typically associated with a specific crisis may be missed because questions are not asked. Symptoms may also be misinterpreted due to cultural differences, unless the instrument has been validated using people from different cultures (Prediger, 1994). The sheer number of these instruments also limits their usefulness, because crisis workers may have time to familiarize themselves with only a few of them.

Another method of gathering information during the assessment process in crisis intervention, though not as common, involves the use of standardized personality tests, which can be adapted for use in crisis intervention. Questions can be edited or deleted to focus and/or shorten the test. Either of these procedures jeopardizes the reliability and validity of the instrument, requiring a revalidation of the revised instrument. A second, more common practice is to modify the interpretations of the results for crisis situations. This method can help crisis workers identify issues that may be indirectly affecting clients' reactions. However, crisis workers may also be flooded with too much information, some of which may violate clients' right to privacy. For example, test results may suggest a client is experiencing sexual identity problems that have no relationship to the crisis situation that caused the client to seek professional help. This information could improperly influence the intervention process unless crisis workers are careful. Also, general personality tests are time-consuming. One agency advocated for the use of the Minnesota Multiphasic Personality Test—which takes a minimum of 1½ hours to complete—in crisis situations. Imagine the experience of clients in crisis coming to an agency only to be told they must complete a test that is 566 questions long, not to mention the time needed for scoring and interpretation. Only a few well-experienced clinicians have the training to interpret these instruments quickly and accurately. Cultural bias is also an issue with standardized instruments (Anastasi & Urbina, 1997). As noted, unless an instrument has been validated with people from different cultures, the results will have limited usefulness.

Of the three assessment practices, the interview seems to be the most serviceable. Crisis workers do not need special training in psychometrics and test interpretation to develop interviewing skills. Yet, as mentioned previously, crisis workers cannot rely on asking whatever comes to mind. Training is needed in order to understand how to ask questions and what to look for. This training should involve learning an assessment model that will guide crisis workers as they gather information and develop intervention strategies for clients in crisis (Hoff, 1995).

ASSESSMENT MODELS

Accurate assessment is the key to effective crisis intervention (Greenstone & Leviton, 1993). Many elements must be evaluated quickly, often within the first 5 minutes of the intervention. Using minimal information, crisis workers must make decisions regarding the focus of the intervention, the best approach to use, and the level of care needed to ensure clients' safety. Complicating the matter, crisis workers may have just met a client or may be talking with the person on the phone, creating even more of a burden due to the limited contact. According to Dale (1995), the key elements in gathering information on the telephone are confidence in what is being said and patience in dealing with the caller. By using good communication and listening skills, crisis workers can obtain the information needed to assess clients. At times, the situation may also involve life or death, as in cases involving suicidal clients, domestic violence, and child abuse. Crisis workers must be adept at identifying relevant material and ignoring details that will only hinder the intervention. Care must be taken to ensure that the proper procedures are used to ensure client safety in these situations.

Having a general assessment model or framework can help crisis workers structure their approach to gathering information in a crisis situation (Hendricks & McKean, 1995, Hoff, 1995). To be useful, however, the model must meet several guidelines. The more completely an assessment model fits these guidelines, the more practical the model is.

First, an assessment model should be parsimonious and user friendly. Crisis workers should feel confident that they can easily recall and apply the model while working with clients. Complicated and involved models lead to frustration at best; at worst, crisis workers will not pay attention to clients because they are focusing on the model they are supposed to be following. Second, the model should be adaptable for use with many types of crisis situations. Even crisis workers who work in agencies specializing in one type of crisis (e.g., domestic violence shelters, rape trauma centers, etc.) are sometimes asked to work with clients experiencing other types of crises. If crisis workers only know a model tailored to a specific crisis, their ability to respond effectively will be reduced. Third, the model needs to be holistic, considering all aspects of clients in their experience of the crisis situation (Greenstone & Leviton, 1993). Too often, crisis workers concentrate on only one part of the client's reactions to the crisis situation. Failing to recognize that a crisis involves more than an emotional reaction, for example, may lead to ineffective and potentially damaging treatment, including long-term psychological problems (James & Gilliland, 2001). Fourth, the model must be appropriate for the time-limited nature of the crisis situation and guide the intervention process (Slaikeu, 1990). Too often crisis workers are distracted from resolving the immediate crisis because they are focusing on gathering information that may not be relevant to the crisis at hand. Fifth, the assessment model must recognize that people from different cultures react differently to crisis events (Irish, 1993). Respect for cultural heritage is critical in the assessment process. If crisis workers are unaware of the cultural element, they may label a client's reaction pathological when, in fact, the reaction is normative for that client's culture. Finally, an assessment model for crisis intervention should be fluid and continually usable during the intervention process. Successful intervention depends on crisis workers being able to assess clients' reactions as these are being expressed. In this sense, the focus of assessment should be present oriented. Yet on the one hand, as Burgess and Baldwin (1981) state, clients' past experiences cannot be completely ignored because they may be critical in helping them to resolve the current crisis. On

TABLE
2.1   **MODELS OF CRISIS ASSESSMENT**

	Vulnerability Model (Hoff, 1995)	Multidimensional Model (Slaikeu, 1990)	Frontline Model (Hendricks & McKean, 1995)	Triage Assessment Model (Myer et al., 1992)
Parsimonious/ user-friendly	weak	weak	weak	strong
Adaptability	strong	strong	weak	strong
Holistic	strong	strong	strong	strong
Guide for intervention	weak	weak	weak	strong
Cultural sensitivity	strong	strong	weak	strong
Fluidity and usability on ongoing basis	strong	weak	strong	strong

the other hand, crisis workers must not allow clients' past experiences to become the focal point of the assessment. The most useful time to explore clients' past experiences is when ideas are generated during treatment to resolve the current crisis.

Table 2.1 compares four different assessment models in terms of the guidelines described above. These models represent perspectives from different human service fields. The first two models, Hoff (1995) and Slaikeu (1990), reflect a traditional mental health perspective but from different disciplines—Hoff from nursing and Slaikeu from community psychology. The third model, developed by Hendricks and McKean (1995), depicts assessment "on the street." This model is used in the training of groups such as police officers, firefighters, victim assistance workers, and others who may come in contact with people in crisis.

Hoff Model

Hoff (1995) contends that assessment involves two levels: (a) safety and (b) the ability to function. Level 1 involves determining if the threat of harm is present. This threat may be in the form of suicidal ideations or homicidal intent. Level 2 assessment involves consideration of personal and social characteristics of the person in crisis.

Hoff's (1995) model can best be described as a "vulnerability model." To assess vulnerability, crisis workers must consider three elements: (a) the hazardous event, (b) the precipitating factor, and (c) the person's reaction. These elements interact to result in a crisis reaction. The *hazardous event* is "the initial shock that sets in motion a series of reactions culminating in a crisis" (Hoff, 1995, p. 79). According to Hoff, this event is not enough to cause a crisis reaction, but rather sets the stage for a crisis. Because the event is unusual in terms of timing, severity, or because it stretches a person's ability to cope, it sets the stage for a crisis, but does not necessarily precipitate one. If the person involved is able to recognize the potential for crisis at this time, he or she may avoid a full-blown crisis reaction by seeking the appropriate help. The *precipitating factor* is what tips the scales toward crisis. It may be that a hazardous event has occurred, depleting the person's resources. Then, a minor accident occurs, taking on crisis proportions because the necessary resources are unavailable.

Hoff borrows the term *crisis plumage* from Hansell (1976) to describe the *person's reaction,* the third segment of the assessment process. Assessing the crisis plumage involves examining distress signals:

1. Difficulty in managing feelings
2. Suicidal or homicidal behaviors
3. Alcohol or other substance abuse
4. Trouble with the law
5. Inability to effectively use available assistance (Hoff, 1995)

According to Hoff, these signals may be affective, cognitive, or behavioral and must be differentiated from distorted perceptions associated with mental illness. Affective reactions may include anxiety, fear, anger, shame, or guilt. Cognitive signs are the inability to utilize problem-solving skills and also a limited loss of memory about the event. Behavioral indices are changes in the ability to perform normal vocational functions, withdrawal from social interactions, and lack of impulse control.

Hoff (1995) also suggests gathering information on a person's assets and liabilities with respect to family and social resources. This layer of assessment can help crisis workers identify cultural and socioeconomic factors impacting the crisis situation, along with family issues that may be contributing to the crisis. In addition, assessment of the family and community components may suggest possible resources a person can mobilize to help during the crisis.

Hoff's (1995) model has several strengths. First, it is comprehensive. Hoff attempts to consider as many variables as possible that may be contributing to a reaction. Second, she emphasizes that cultural factors are important in understanding clients' reactions to crisis events. Third, the model appears to be adaptable to all crisis situations and can be used throughout treatment to monitor clients' progress. Finally, Hoff includes a sample intake form that crisis workers can use to record information and possible treatment recommendations.

However, the very comprehensiveness of Hoff's (1995) model makes it somewhat cumbersome to use. The result is that the model becomes unstructured and cluttered, making it difficult to keep track of the information. In addition, the model is weak on directing the intervention process. Hoff's intake form is too general and lacks a direct connection to the intervention process. She does include a more comprehensive form, but this form is 5 pages long and contains too many items for a crisis worker to monitor mentally.

Slaikeu Model

Slaikeu's (1990) crisis assessment involves two stages: assessment for "psychological first-aid" and "crisis therapy." Psychological first-aid is short term and used to help clients reestablish immediate coping. The safety of clients is ensured, and clients are linked with resources for immediate needs. Crisis therapy, on the other hand, extends psychological first-aid by helping clients rebuild their lives after the crisis event, assisting them to work through the crisis and integrate any changes brought on by the crisis event into their lives. Assessment, therefore, is conducted accordingly at the level needed to gather information to develop appropriate interventions.

Slaikeu (1990) proposes a multidimensional model that assesses the affective, behavioral, physical, and cognitive aspects of crisis reactions. This model modifies Lazarus' (1981) BASIC-ID assessment approach, categorizing substance abuse as behavioral rather than in a separate category, characterizing all physical functioning factors (vision, touch, hearing, taste, smell) as somatic functioning, and combining the imagery and cognitive dimensions into one category. Slaikeu (1990) uses the acronym BASIC; *B* represents behavioral aspects of crisis reactions and involves assessing changes in clients' typical day-to-day functioning as well as suicidal or homicidal tendencies. Clients' affective reaction is represented by the *A*, and assessment involves gathering information regarding feelings about current behaviors, the presence of feelings caused by the crisis event and whether these are appropriate to life circumstances, and finally, whether the feelings are hidden or expressed. The *S* stands for somatic issues and involves assessment of general physical functioning, with special attention to the presence or absence of tics, headaches, stomach difficulties, tension, and changes in sensitivity of the five senses since the crisis event. Clients' interpersonal relationships are represented by the *I;* assessment focuses on changes in the nature of relationships, frequency of contact, role taken (e.g., passive, aggressive, etc.), and style of interactions (e.g., suspicious, manipulative, or dependent). Issues such as relationships with family, friends, neighbors, and co-workers are assessed in order to understand clients in the context of their culture and environment. *C* refers to the cognitive aspects of clients' reactions in crisis situations. Emphasis is placed on assessing clients' full range of thoughts and particularly self-statements made about behavior, feelings, and physical functioning. According to Slaikeu, this assessment process produces concrete guidelines that allow crisis workers to develop treatment strategies.

Slaikeu (1990) also offers a checklist to ensure gathering the information needed to help clients in crisis. This checklist is straightforward and includes the precipitating event, the presenting problem, the context of the crisis, pre-crisis BASIC functioning, and crisis BASIC functioning. Slaikeu suggests gathering this information from a variety of sources, such as clients, family members, and referral sources, using an interview format. In addition, Slaikeu has developed a 12-page form to be completed by crisis workers that covers the areas to be assessed.

Like the vulnerability model suggested by Hoff (1995), Slaikeu's (1990) multidimensional model is holistic. Slaikeu's model also is adaptable across a range of crisis situations and can be used during treatment to monitor progress. In addition, the model attempts to be user-friendly through the use of the BASIC assessment approach; but it has shortcomings in this area. While the information is valuable, the form used to record the necessary information is too long and could be difficult to complete in crisis situations. Most crisis workers would have to complete the form outside the session or run the risk of focusing too much on the form and sacrificing rapport with the client by filling out the form during the session. The length and complexity of the form also weakens the link to treatment and makes quick translation to treatment difficult.

Hendricks and McKean Model

Hendricks and McKean's (1995) "frontline model" for assessment in crisis intervention was developed for use on the streets. According to these authors, the assessment process involves two phases: securing the scene and evaluating the person in crisis. First contact with someone in crisis may be when workers are dispatched to the scene of an accident or crime, or it may be by chance, for example, when police officers happen on an automobile accident. The primary object in this phase is to secure the crisis scene. Crisis workers are encouraged to gather as much information as possible prior to arriving on the crisis scene, including facts regarding the situation as well as the identity of whoever is in crisis. Hendricks and McKean suggest crisis workers attempt to formulate questions using "who, what, when, where, and why" as a strategy to obtain the information needed to intervene. They caution that the surroundings and circumstance will dictate the intervention process. Since some situations may involve elements of danger, gathering information prior to arrival on the scene may help to protect everyone, including crisis workers.

Crisis workers should first evaluate the danger of the situation, according to Hendricks and McKean (1995). Crisis workers cannot attend to listening and helping if they feel unsafe. They should pay special attention to any circumstance that may pose a threat. For example, in domestic violence situations, a good strategy is to separate as far as possible everyone involved (Greenstone & Leviton (1993). Crisis workers should also check for the presence of weapons; they also might ask whether the person in crisis has been violent, and if so, when. Are there environmental threats such as downed power lines or other life-threatening situations? Suicidal ideations or homicidal intent must also be evaluated. In short, crisis workers take control of the scene in order to ensure their safety along with that of everyone involved.

In the first phase of the "frontline model," crisis workers must also determine if anyone is injured. Special training is needed to make judgments regarding the seriousness of injuries; therefore, such assessments should be performed only by those who are qualified.

If possible, crisis workers are also encouraged to move people in crisis from the immediate scene. For example, in an automobile accident, move the person away from the immediate area (unless he or she is injured). Hendricks and McKean (1995) believe this procedure is best used when people are experiencing anxiety regarding the crisis.

The second phase of this assessment model involves evaluating the person in crisis—determining people's level of functioning and gathering information regarding their medical and psychiatric history. Questions with respect to how well a person is oriented to time, place, and people should be asked. Are there any medical conditions that might explain someone's behavior? What is the range and intensity of emotion, along with the general mood of the person in crisis? What was the precrisis level of functioning? And finally, is the person under the influence of any chemical, such as alcohol, or prescribed medication, or street drug? The answers to these questions should allow crisis workers to take control of the situation and make appropriate interventions.

Like the other models, Hendricks and McKean's (1995) frontline model for crisis assessment attempts to be holistic by including the environment and person. However, unlike Hoff's (1995) and Slaikeu's (1990) model, this model highlights environmental assessment while glossing over assessment of the person. The reason for this emphasis appears to be the kinds of crisis situations these authors are discussing—accidents and crime scenes. The model is fluid and can be used throughout the intervention. And, the model is simple and easy to follow. However, it lacks the specificity needed to guide the intervention process. While Hendricks and McKean start well by encouraging crisis workers to evaluate the environment and take steps accordingly to ensure the safety of clients as well themselves, they fall short in demonstrating how to translate the information gathered to develop intervention strategies. In addition, they do not specifically discuss the role of culture in the assessment process. This oversight might be explained by the type of crisis they are discussing, yet it would seem that culture would be an important factor in the assessment of crisis on the frontline. Several other general suggestions are made about what information should be obtained, but more is needed for crisis workers to know how to use this material.

An apparent weakness shared by these models is that they are cumbersome. As noted, the model should facilitate the efficient and effective gathering of information, but with these assessment models, crisis workers may find themselves concentrating on completing forms associated with the model rather than listening to clients, which will have a negative impact on outcome. The triage assessment model overcomes these drawbacks, particularly in the areas of guiding treatment and being user-friendly. As you read about this model, I encourage you to think about ways to adapt and use it in your work.

TRIAGE ASSESSMENT MODEL

The triage assessment model (TDA; Myer, Williams, Ottens, & Schmidt, 1992) for crisis intervention shown in Figure 2.1 can assist crisis workers in understanding clients' reactions during a crisis. This model assumes that it is necessary to assess crisis reactions in three domains: affective (emotional), cognitive (thinking), and behavioral (actions). In addition, the TDA helps crisis workers identify the complex interaction among these domains. Individual client reactions are unique to the clients and to the situation. Assessing clients along these three domains helps to capture the complexity of the crisis situation. Of course, as with any assessment approach, crisis workers need to be aware of cultural

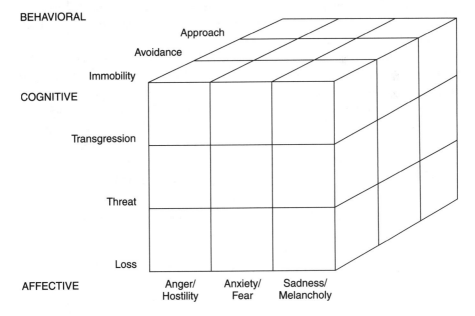

FIGURE 2.1
Triage Assessment Model

Myer, R. A., Williams, R. C., Ottens, A J., & Schmidt, A. E. (1992). Crisis assessment: A three dimensional model for triage. *Journal of Mental Health Counseling, 14,* 137–148. Used by permission of the *Journal of Mental Health Counseling.*

differences; the same reactions do not necessarily mean the same thing across cultures.

Each dimension is divided into three types of responses that represent the range of reactions clients experience in crisis situations for that particular domain. The affective domain includes anger/hostility, anxiety/fear, and sadness/melancholy. Clients are assessed to determine the presence of these three emotions and which is the primary reaction. The TDA defines cognitive reactions as clients' perception of the event and the areas of their life affected by the crisis. These are categorized into a perception of a transgression, a threat, and a loss. Transgression refers to the client's perception of violation and is couched in the present. Clients perceive a transgression when their rights are being violated by someone not behaving in a socially acceptable way. For example, an employer may be making suggestive comments or even demanding physical intimacy with an employee. Clients experiencing a threat judge that the event has the potential to harm them in some area of their lives. Clients experiencing this reaction will be focused on the future and what may happen as a result of the crisis situation. In contrast, loss refers to a belief that the crisis has caused something to be irretrievable. Clients believe the object or relationship to be gone forever, with no hope of recovering it. Clients may perceive a transgression, threat, or loss in each of the following life dimensions: (a) physical (health, shelter, safety), (b) psychological (self-concept, identity, and emotional well-being), (c) social relationships (with family, friends, co-workers), and (d) moral/spiritual (personal integrity, values, and belief system).

Reactions in the behavioral domain include approach, avoidance, and immobility. Clients will be primarily reacting using one of these three behaviors with respect to attempting to resolve the crisis. Approach behaviors are either overt or covert attempts to address the crisis event. Avoidance behaviors ignore, evade, or escape the crisis event. Immobility refers to behaviors that are nonproductive, disorganized, or self-defeating attempts to cope with the crisis. Each of these approaches to coping may be either constructive or maladaptive (Myer & Ottens, 1991). For example, a person who is being harassed at work may display constructive avoidance behavior by having his or her telephone number unlisted and avoiding areas where the harassment is taking place; but to stop going to work altogether would be maladaptive.

The TDA has been operationalized through the development of the Triage Assessment Form: Crisis Intervention (TAF; Myer, Williams, Ottens, & Schmidt, 1991). See Appendix B for a copy of the TAF. This form includes a severity scale for each domain. Initially, treatment should address the most severe reaction. Because the severity of the reaction varies throughout the crisis event and treatment, crisis workers are advised to adjust the intervention to meet clients' needs. Results from the severity scales also suggest how directive the intervention should be. The higher the score, the more directive the intervention. This permits crisis workers to address salient needs in a manner appropriate to the severity of the reaction. More will be said about the severity scales in Chapters 3, 4, and 5.

Results from research on the reliability and validity of the TAF are promising. In an independent research project, Watters (1997) concluded the TAF is reliable and valid, especially for crisis workers with minimal experience. In this study, four groups were trained to use the TAF and presented with videotaped vignettes. The groups consisted of inexperienced students at the undergraduate and graduate levels, police academy recruits, experienced graduate students enrolled in a counseling program, and experienced crisis intervention personnel. The vignettes were role-played with a person who was in crisis and a crisis worker. Developed to represent varying degrees of the same issue, these were shown to the participants after they had been trained in using the TAF. The results of their assessment were compared with each other and experts in the crisis intervention. Reliability coefficients on interrater reliability varied from a low of .53 to a high of .79 on the most severe vignette, from .63 to .86 for the vignette representing a moderate reaction to a crisis, and from .65 to .94 for the vignette that represented the least severe reaction. These results are quite high since even the low coefficient—.53 on the most severe vignette—manifests a 97% agreement with the experts. Watters, therefore, concluded that the vignettes have satisfactory interrater reliability.

Watters (1997) established the TAF's validity by comparing the average rating of the groups with that of experts in crisis intervention. Three experts were chosen for their familiarity with the TAF and asked to assess the vignettes. The percentage of agreement between the mean ratings of the experts and the groups for each vignette were calculated in order to determine the validity of the TAF. The threshold of agreement was set at 75% to affirm the validity of the TAF. Inexperienced undergraduate and graduate students agreed on each vignette with the experts, while police recruits and experienced graduate students agreed with the experts on two of the three vignettes. The fourth group, experienced crisis intervention personnel, did not agree on any of the vignettes. Watters attributed this to the fact that (a) the experienced crisis workers did not even agree among themselves, and (b) the members of this group had quite varied levels of experience and training. Further, Watters surmised that the training they received in the TAF did not overcome previous training and experience using other assessment models. Although the results of this portion of the study were not as strong as with the interrater reliability, Watters concluded that the TAF is valid. However, she did suggest that care be used in training crisis workers to use the TAF by adjusting the training according to the level of expertise and experience of the trainee.

In conclusion, the TDA/TAF meets the criteria for assessment models suggested earlier in this chapter. First, this model and assessment form are parsimonious and user-friendly. Also, the triage assessment model outlining the domains to be assessed is easily remembered and used during the intervention process. Second, research conducted on the TAF indicates that the model is reliable and valid for use in a variety of crisis situations (Watters, 1997). Third, the TDA/TAF is holistic. This model and the assessment instrument address the interaction of clients' reactions across affective, cognitive, and behavioral domains. In addition, the TAF assesses the life dimension(s) (physical, psychological, social relationships, and moral/spiritual) affected by the crisis. This comprehensiveness gives crisis workers a structure to understand clients and prevents crisis workers from neglecting or missing important information. Fourth, the intervention process is directed by the TAF. The severity scales of this instrument can be used as a guidepost in the intervention process for crisis workers, clearly linking the model to treatment. Finally, the TDA/TAF is fluid and usable throughout treatment. Clients' reactions will change and evolve during treatment. For example, clients may initially react very emotionally to a crisis, but after a few days or possibly a few minutes, their reaction might change, with the affective reaction decreasing and the cognitive or behavioral reaction becoming more severe. Crisis workers can use the TDA/TAF to understand these switches and adapt their intervention techniques accordingly.

SUMMARY

Of the methods to assess people in crisis, the interview is the most often used. The interview, however, must be based on a model that enhances crisis workers' ability to gather germane, accurate information. The model must be easily used and flexible, permitting crisis workers to attain information about clients' reactions in all areas of their life. In addition, the intervention process should be guided by the information that has been obtained. The model should also allow ongoing assessment throughout the intervention. In this way, crisis workers can continually adapt the intervention to clients' needs. As noted, the model that appears to best meet these criteria is the triage assessment model. This model and the accompanying Triage Assessment Form enable crisis workers to collect information regarding clients' affective, cognitive, and behavioral reactions. This model also helps identify the area needing immediate attention and how direct the intervention should be.

POINTS TO REMEMBER

- Of the three most common practices for assessing clients in crisis, the interview is the most often utilized. The other two practices involve the use of crisis-specific standardized inventories and general personality tests that are interpreted in light of the crisis.

- Assessment interviews are on a continuum from structured to unstructured. Two problems associated with interviews involve (a) being too scattered, or using a "shotgun" approach that risks missing relevant information, and (b) being too narrowly focused, resulting in the failure to gather information needed to resolve the crisis. A strategy to avoid these problems is the utilization of an assessment model that guides the interview.
- Assessment models should be
  Parsimonious—uncomplicated and simple to use
  Adaptable—usable across crisis situations
  Holistic—considering the broader context of clients' experience and reactions related to the crisis
  A guide for the intervention—maintaining crisis workers' focus on the immediate problem as well as directing the intervention process
  Sensitive to cultural differences—recognizing that reactions to crises vary across cultures
  Usable throughout the intervention—allowing crisis workers to assess clients' fluctuating reactions to the evolving situation
- The triage assessment model posits that clients' reactions fall into three domains: (a) affective, (b) cognitive, and (c) behavioral.
- Affective reactions include (a) anger/hostility, (b) anxiety/fear, and (c) sadness/melancholy.
- Cognitive reactions include (a) transgression, (b) threat, and (c) loss. Four life dimensions may be affected by cognitive reactions—physical, psychological, social relationships, and moral/spiritual issues.
- Behavioral reactions include (a) approach, (b) avoidance, and (c) immobility, and can be either constructive or maladaptive.

STUDY QUESTIONS

1. List advantages and disadvantages of the three main crisis assessment methods presented in this chapter (i.e., specialized self-report instrument, personality tests, and interviews).
2. Using the case of Amy described at the beginning of the chapter, summarize how you would assess her using a specialized self-report instrument, personality test, and interview. What would you expect each of these to tell you?
3. Why is having an assessment model critical in crisis assessment?
4. How would having a model of assessment help you understand what Amy is experiencing?
5. How might your culture influence how you react in a crisis?

REFERENCES

Anastasi, A., & Urbina, S. (1997). *Psychological testing* (7th ed.). Upper Saddle River, NJ: Prentice-Hall.

Bernstein, D. P., & Fink, L. (1997). Childhood trauma questionnaire manual. San Antonio, TX: The Psychological Corporation.

Booner, R. L. (1990). A "M.A.P." to the clinical assessment of suicide risk. *Journal of Mental Health Counseling, 12,* 232–236.

Burgess, A. W., & Baldwin, B. A. (1981). *Crisis intervention theory and practice: A clinical handbook.* Englewood Cliffs, NJ: Prentice-Hall.

Crow, G. (1977). *Crisis intervention.* New York: Association Press.

Dale, J. (1995). Development of telephone advice in A & E: Establishing the views of staff. *Nursing Standard, 9,* 28–31.

Durlak, J. A., & Roth, J. A. (1983). Use of paraprofessionals in crisis intervention. In L. H. Cohen, W. L. Claiborn, & G. A. Specter (Eds.), *Crisis intervention* (2nd. ed., pp. 33–54). New York: Human Science Press.

Greenstone, J. L., & Leviton, S. C. (1993). *Elements of crisis intervention: Crises and how to respond to them.* Pacific Grove, CA: Brooks/Cole.

Hansell, N. (1976). *The person in distress.* New York: Human Services Press.

Hendricks, J. E., & McKean, J. B. (1995). *Crisis intervention: Contemporary issues for on-site interveners.* Springfield, IL: Charles C. Thomas Publishers.

Hinkle, J. S. (1994). Practitioners and cross-cultural assessment: A practical guide to information and training. *Measurement and Evaluation in Counseling and Development, 27,* 103–115.

Hoff, L. A. (1995). *People in crisis: Understanding and helping* (4th. ed.). Redwood City, CA: Addison-Wesley.

Irish, D. P. (1993). Multiculturalism and the majority population. In D. P. Irish, K. F. Lundquist, & V. J. Nelson (Eds.), *Ethnic variations in dying, death, and grief: Diversity in universality* (pp. 1–12). Washington DC: Taylor & Francis.

Jackson, T. L., & Ferguson, W. (1983). Attribution of blame in incest. *American Journal of Community Psychology, 11,* 313–322.

James, R. K., & Gilliland, B. E. (2001). *Crisis intervention strategies* (4th. ed.). Monterey, CA: Brooks/Cole.

Keane, T. M., Caddell, J. M., & Taylor, K. L. (1988). Mississippi Scale for combat related post-traumatic stress disorder: Three studies in reliability and validity. *Journal of Consulting and Clinical Psychology, 56,* 85–90.

Lazarus, A. A. (1981). *The practice of multimodel therapy.* New York: McGraw-Hill Books.

Myer, R. A., & Ottens, A. J. (1994). Assessment for crisis intervention on college campuses. *Crisis Intervention and Time Limited Treatment, 1,* 31–46.

Myer, R. A., Williams, R. C., Ottens, A. J., & Schmidt, A. E. (1992). Crisis assessment: A three-dimensional model for triage. *Journal of Mental Health Counseling, 14,* 137–148.

Myer, R. A., Williams, R. C., Ottens, A. J., & Schmidt, A. E. (1991). Triage assessment form: Crisis intervention. Unpublished manuscript, Northern Illinois University, Department of Counseling, Educational Psychology, and Special Education, DeKalb, IL.

Prediger, D. J. (1994). Multicultural assessment standards: A compilation for counselors. *Measurement and Evaluation in Counseling and Development, 27,* 68–73.

Psychological Assessment Resources. (2000, January). *Catalog of professional resources,* volume 23. Odessa, FL: Psychological Assessment Resources, Inc.

The Psychological Corporation. (2000). *Catalog for psychological assessment and intervention products.* San Antonio, TX: The Psychological Corporation.

Resnick, P. A., Veronen, L. J., Kilpatrick, D. G., Calhoun, K. S., & Atkeson, B. M. (1986). Assessment of fear reactions in sexual assault victims: A factor analytic study of the Veronen-Kilpatrick Modified Fear Survey. *Behavioral Assessment, 8,* 271–283.

Saylor, C. F., Swenson, C. C., Reynolds, S. S., & Taylor, M. (1999). The Pediatric Emotional Distress Scale: A brief screening measure for young children exposed to traumatic events. *Journal of Clinical Child Psychology, 28,* 70–81.

Slaikeu, K. A. (1990). *Crisis intervention: A handbook for practice and research* (2nd. ed.). Boston: Allyn and Bacon.

Watters, D. S. (1997). *A study of the reliability and validity of the Triage Assessment Scale.* Dissertation Abstracts.

ASSESSMENT OF AFFECTIVE REACTIONS

Sandy is a 43-year-old married woman with three children—a boy age 13 and two girls ages 16 and 20. She called the mental health agency one morning asking for an appointment as soon as possible for the purpose of figuring out a way to tell her family that she may have lung cancer. Sandy was assigned a crisis worker and given an appointment that afternoon. When she arrived, Sandy was taken to the crisis worker's office. Upon seeing Sandy, the crisis worker observed that her clothing appeared disheveled and that her hair was not combed. The crisis worker also noticed that Sandy smelled like cigarette smoke and asked if she smoked. Sandy responded slowly, in a low tone of voice, that she did smoke. During the session, Sandy sat quietly with her hands folded, answering questions with seemingly as few words as possible. At times, the crisis worker noticed that Sandy's responses seemed distant, almost like she was talking about someone else. At other times, Sandy spoke hurriedly, using what seemed to be a normal tone of voice when discussing the diagnosis. Sandy said that her physician had told her of her suspicion of lung cancer five days before, and wanted to confirm the diagnosis. Sandy stated that at first, she could hardly believe the diagnosis could be true, but that the physician was concerned and wanted to do a biopsy as soon as possible. Sandy stated she had not told her family because she did not want to alarm them.

To identify Sandy's affective or feeling reaction to learning she may have lung cancer, the crisis worker must be attentive to many details. Sandy's verbal and nonverbal behavior communicates loudly that she has mixed emotions regarding this crisis. Sandy's choice of not talking with her family about the problem is also important. Why is she reluctant to turn to her family? Could the actual crisis be something other than the suspected illness? Finally, it is significant that Sandy demanded to have an appointment immediately. Using this information will enable the crisis worker to accurately identify Sandy's affective reaction to the crisis situation.

This chapter will help crisis workers learn to assess clients' affective reactions to crisis situations. As noted in Chapter 2, the affective reactions include anger/hostility, anxiety/fear, and sadness/melancholy. First, I will give an overview of crisis workers' role in assessing feelings, highlighting potential problems and giving suggestions about how to avoid them. Second, I will describe the range of affective reactions people may have in crisis situations, offering practical suggestions and guidelines for evaluating them and gauging their severity.

CRISIS WORKERS' ROLE

Because crisis situations are generally affect laden (Dixon, 1979), crisis workers must prepare themselves for listening to extreme emotional expressions from clients. Clients may scream in rage or sob uncontrollably. Clients may also be numb and find it difficult to vocalize any feelings. Or, clients may direct their feelings at crisis workers by lashing out in anger. If not prepared, crisis workers may be bewildered by clients' display of feelings. The intensity of clients' emotional expression may result in crisis workers feeling uncomfortable and out of control. As a result, crisis workers may attempt to shift attention away from these emotions by consoling clients or prematurely shifting clients' attention away from these feelings. Crisis workers must be able to tolerate clients' affective reactions and be prepared to support clients through the venting of these feelings.

Expression of Emotions

First, crisis workers must be aware that the expression of emotional reactions to crisis events is healthy. In Lindemann's (1944) work with survivors of the Coconut Grove nightclub fire of 1943, he discovered that premature cessation of the expression of feelings is harmful. Recent research supports this finding, showing that closing off or ignoring emotional reactions to a crisis may result in long-term mental health issues (James & Gilliland, 2001; Schwartz, 1997). Therefore, it is essential for crisis workers to allow the expression of emotional reactions to a crisis. However, crisis workers must also ensure that the expression of these feelings is not harmful to the client or others (Kleespies, Deleppo, Mori, & Niles, 1998). Crisis workers must help clients manage the venting of affect in a supportive and safe environment. For example, when I was working in an emergency room (ER) at a general hospital, a family exploded in emotion after learning that their mother had died. They ran up and down the hallways, entering treatment rooms trying to find their mother. After physically restraining several family members, a security officer and I set specific guidelines for the expression of feelings to ensure the safety of the family as well as others in the ER. The family was told that under no circumstances would they be allowed to run around the ER again. I stated that they must respect other patients and families in the ER and allow the medical staff to do their work. In addition, the family was told that any more disruptive behaviors would result in the security guard escorting them off hospital grounds. For the next two hours I talked with the family, helping them to express their emotions and begin the grief process. At various points, family members would express intense emotional reactions. At one point, a nurse and I escorted the family to the room in which the mother lay. The family prayed and began the process of saying goodbye to their mother. The challenge is to find the balance between allowing the expression of emotion without putting the clients or others at risk of harm.

Sharing Client's Pain

Second, crisis workers must be willing to share the client's pain—to empathize (Caplan, 1964; Dixon, 1979; James & Gilliland, 2001; Lindemann, 1944). Empathy demonstrates to clients that crisis workers understand their frame of reference in the crisis situation. This is not to say crisis workers must have experienced the same crisis as a client (James & Gilliland, 2001; rather, crisis workers must be able to use their experience and training to "feel what the client feels." At the same time, crisis workers must guard against overinvolvement with clients, which can be counterproductive and even harmful (James & Gilliland, 2001; Kennedy, 1981). Crisis workers must find a neutral ground that allows them to understand clients' affective reactions while maintaining a safe professional distance (Kennedy, 1981).

Maintaining the balance between empathy and overinvolvement is not easy. By definition, a crisis is when clients' typical coping mechanisms or resources are inadequate to resolve the situation; thus they are generally very needy and may be incapable of helping themselves. At times, therefore, crisis workers may allow and even encourage some dependence as they help clients through a crisis; but they must be careful not to cultivate undue dependence (Bloom, 1984). Instead, crisis workers must assist clients but at the same time look for opportunities to empower them to resolve the situation themselves. Signs of overdependence include such things as frequent phone calls, unexpected visits, deference to crisis workers' authority in matters unrelated to the crisis, and clients stating they are in love with the crisis worker. Crisis workers should monitor clients' dependence through periodic consultation and supervision, developing a step-by-step plan to wean clients if necessary. This plan should consider the intensity of the crisis event along with the level of clients' reaction. No formula exists to determine the degree and length of dependence that is appropriate.

Since the crisis is the client's perception, each case must be considered individually.

Crisis Workers' Emotional Reaction

Third, crisis workers should be aware of their own emotional reactions when helping clients (James & Gilliland, 2001; Kennedy, 1981). Care must be used to guard against allowing crisis workers' personal issues to influence the assessment process. For example, a crisis worker, while a child, may have seen his or her mother abused by the father or another person. As a result, the crisis worker may become angry whenever abuse is an issue. This crisis worker must be mindful in the assessment process to distinguish his or her feelings from the client's. Not all clients react with anger to being abused; some may react emotionally by experiencing anxiety or sadness. If the crisis worker allows his or her feeling to impact the assessment process, the intervention will likely be ineffective.

This issue has ethical implications; all ethical codes caution against allowing personal issues and feelings to inappropriately influence any intervention with clients (e.g., American Counseling Association, 1995; American Psychological Association, 1992; see also Appendix A). Since many crisis workers are volunteers, application of a professional organization's ethical standards may be difficult. Although training for volunteers should include ethical and legal issues, many crisis workers may be unaware of specific ethical standards. As a general rule, crisis workers should be wary when intervening with clients who have problems the same or similar to their own, being careful to use their own experiences to understand the client's situation without imposing their own feelings and interpretations.

AFFECTIVE REACTIONS

The rise of affect to uncomfortable levels is a hallmark sign of a person in crisis (Baldwin, 1979). These affective reactions range from negligible to extremely severe and can cause an instability that jeopardizes a person's psychological homeostatic balance (Caplan, 1964). Lindemann (1944, 1956) pioneered the research on affective reactions to a crisis through his work with survivors of the Coconut Grove nightclub fire, which killed 492 people. Although Lindemann targeted people's reactions to a sudden loss and subsequent grief, his work can be generalized to all crisis situations (Hoff, 1995). Lindemann found that survivors of the tragedy who for whatever reason failed to experience normal grieving close to the time of the fire developed significant psychological disturbances. Lindemann helped professionals and paraprofessionals recognize that while reactions to crisis situations may seem pathological, they are normal, temporary, and amenable to alleviation using short-term intervention strategies (James & Gilliland, 2001).

Many authors have written about the connection between people's affective reactions and crisis situations, although research efforts are fraught with difficulties because emotions are expressed primarily through language, and language is not easily pinned down (National Advisory Mental Health Council, 1995). In the English language, hundreds of words and phrases can be used to describe feelings. Other complications arise when one considers the evolution of the meaning of words, the developmental stage of the person using a word, the situation in which words are used, the use of colloquialisms and phrases to express emotions, and cultural factors. In spite of these challenges, research examining emotions has a rich, long history of systematic inquiry. One line of inquiry explores the belief that there is a small number of primary or basic emotions—a limited number of prototypical emotions that are the building blocks of all feelings. This concept stems from philosophical literature that characterizes emotions as either primary or secondary, and generally is widely accepted in the field of crisis intervention (Plutchick, 1980). According to Plutchick, primary emotions are feelings shared by both people and other animals (e.g., joy, anger, fear, and love). Primary emotions are also adaptive, relating to basic biological processes that promote survival and the avoidance of harm. In addition, primary emotions involve a whole-body reaction as opposed to just thought. Secondary emotions, on the other hand, are mixtures of primary emotions; as varying degrees or intensity levels of primary are experienced, new emotions emerge that are more or less hybrids.

Research on primary emotions has followed several avenues, examining (a) infant reactions, adult self-reports, and cross-cultural variations in expression (National Advisory Mental Health Council, 1995); (b) animals, especially apes, and structural aspects of the brain (Plutchick, 1980); and (c) facial expression (Siegman, 1993). The goal of this research is to determine if primary emotions exist and if so, what they are. The findings have been mixed, but most investigators agree that primary emotions exist, and they typically identify between 6 and 10 primary emotions, some positive and others negative. Emotions identified as positive are those that generate pleasant feelings and include anticipation, joy, acceptance, love, hope, desire, delight, and surprise, depending on the model (Plutchick, 1980). Negative emotions, on the other hand, create unpleasant or troublesome impressions and include anger, fear, terror, sadness, sorrow, aversion, hate, and disgust (Plutchick, 1980).

Six emotions consistently identified as primary are described in a report published by the National Advisory Mental Health Council (1995): love, joy, and surprise; and anger, anxiety, and sadness.

Lindemann (1944) and Caplan (1964) were among the first to examine the relationship of affective reactions to crises, but stopped short of identifying specific affective reactions. Others have used their work, however, to build their own models. Crow (1977), for example, identified three affective reactions that occur in crises: anger; fear, and sadness. He likened angry reactions to crises to the color "red" and suggested that these reactions have the potential of causing significant problems in a person's life if not addressed. Anger, he stated, lowers people's ability to self-regulate, resulting in an inability to thoughtfully consider the consequences of actions; the angrier people are, the more unable they are to regulate their behavior. This tendency is well documented throughout the literature. Crisis workers are cautioned to be careful with clients who react to a crisis with anger, since they are potentially violent (Eddy & Harris, 1998). Appropriate preparations should be made in order to protect crisis workers in case clients become violent (Eddy & Harris, 1998; Greenstone & Leviton, 1993). Crow used "yellow" to characterize anxiety or fear. He believes this type of reaction is the most typical in crisis situations, because those in crisis become overwhelmed and coping mechanisms become ineffective. Empirical evidence to support this belief is minimal, however. To the contrary, most literature indicates that other emotional reactions are typically observed, depending on situational and personality factors (Hoff, 1995; Roberts, 1996). Crow associated the color "black" with sadness, cautioning that when people react in this manner, crisis workers should watch for suicidal ideations. This caution is well taken, since the feelings of hopelessness and helplessness associated with sadness are also a warning sign of suicide (Kanel, 1999).

The relationship between primary emotions and crisis intervention is intuitive. If a set of primary emotions exists, it is these emotions that will be expressed when a person is in crisis. For example, when a person learns of the tragic death of a family member, he or she does not stop to think about how to feel; rather he or she simply reacts with a feeling. The universality of these feelings also support their use for understanding a person's reactions to a crisis event. These feelings are experienced by all cultures and are therefore well suited for understanding the affective reactions for clients in crisis.

ASSESSMENT OF AFFECTIVE REACTIONS

Of the three types of reactions (i.e., affective, cognitive, and behavioral) clients experience in response to a crisis, identifying clients' affective or feeling reactions is usually the easiest. Many times clients will simply tell crisis workers what they are feeling. They will come to the office or call on the phone and say something like, "I'm scared and don't know what to do," "I am really depressed, I am tired of living," or "I am mad, that shouldn't happen to anyone." These statements make determining the affective reaction much easier, particularly if these are repeated several times during the first few minutes of an interview. Yet, absolute dependence on these kinds of statements can be misleading, because clients' affective reactions typically cycle through all three feelings (anger, anxiety, and sadness) at various times during the crisis. Crisis workers must develop the skill to determine the emotional response that is the primary reaction to the crisis event. In addition, crisis workers must understand that some cultures may use somatic complaints to describe feelings, for example, stating they have stomach pains when they are angry (Egli, Shiota, Ben-Porath, & Butcher, 1991). Attention, therefore, must be given to physical complaints to determine if these are actually descriptions of feelings. Once the primary affective reaction is assessed, crisis workers can focus the intervention to help clients recognize and work through these feelings.

Affect versus Mood

Assessing the dominant affective reaction requires that crisis workers differentiate between *affect* and *mood,* both of which must be examined. *Affect* refers to the prevailing feeling clients experience resulting from a crisis, and is more time limited, whereas *mood* refers to feelings that are more pervasive and sustained over time (Akiskal & Akiskal, 1994). Crisis workers need to be able to recognize clients' primary affect. Clients who are angry, for example, will benefit from techniques that facilitate appropriate catharsis—expression of the anger in such a way that does not harm the client or others physically, emotionally, or economically. On the other hand, anxious clients will gain from strategies that promote a sense of safety. Assessment of mood is important for understanding the severity of clients' affective reaction. The more unstable and changeable the mood, the more severe the reaction. Crisis workers' sensitivity to clients' mood is especially important to determine if harm to self or others is being contemplated. If clients' affective reactions are at a level that destabilizes their mood, they may be at risk for suicide or homicide. In these situations, intervention strategies that promote client safety are necessary.

Using Verbal and Nonverbal Behavior

During the initial contact, crisis workers must observe both verbal and nonverbal behavior in the assessment of clients' affective response, because clients may not express their feelings verbally. For beginning crisis workers, identifying nonverbally expressed emotions can be difficult. However, by practicing being attentive to nonverbal cues and becoming sensitive to what signals are relevant, crisis workers can begin to quickly and accurately recognize the salient affective response.

According to Hackney and Cormier (1994), the affective message is highly dependent on nonverbal signals. Some researchers (e.g., Birdwhistell, 1970) estimate that at least 65% of all communication is conveyed through nonverbal gestures. Table 3.1 lists nonverbal cues that can help crisis workers identify clients' affective reactions. A cautionary note is important at this point. Non-

TABLE
3.1 NONVERBAL CUES AND CORRESPONDING AFFECTIVE REACTIONS

Physiological	Gestural	
Blotchy facial complexion—anger	Mouth	Pursed lips (tight lips)—anger
Pale facial complexion—anxiety		Quivering lips—anxiety or sadness
Contracted pupils—anger		Biting lips—Sadness
Dilated pupils—anxiety		
Bulging or pulsating carotid artery—anger		
Clammy or cold hands—anxiety		
Sweaty palms—anxiety		
Queasiness—anger or anxiety		
Moist eyes—sadness		
Trembling hands—anger or anxiety		
	Head	Hanging or bowed—sadness
		Head back—anger
	Eyes	Darting—anger or anxiety
		Looking around—anger or anxiety
		Squinting—anger
		Empty look—sadness
		No eye contact—sadness
		Fixation—anxiety
		Widening of eyes—anxiety
		Rubbing—anxiety
	Arms and hands	Hands above waist, palms facing inward—anger
		Opening and closing hands—anger
		Closed fist—anger
		Wringing of hands—anxiety
		Rare use of gestures—anger
		Arms folded on chest—anxiety
	Legs and feet	Crossing and uncrossing of legs—anxiety
		Foot tapping—anxiety
		Stiff legs—anxiety
		If standing, rocking from toes to heels—anger

Adapted from Cormier and Cormier (1998), Greenstone and Leviton (1993), and Ouellette (1993).

verbal cues may be culturally bound, so crisis workers should take care to identify nonverbal cues that are physiological responses as opposed to gestures. Physiological responses are less controllable, and therefore less subject to cultural differences. Nonverbal behaviors such as hand gestures and eye contact, however, are more controllable and more likely influenced by culture (Sue & Sue, 1999). Remember that the meaning of gestures varies from culture to culture, person to person, and situation to situation. Relying on "canned" interpretation generally leads to mislabeling affective reactions. For example, clients sitting on their hands could be interpreted as not wanting to disclose feelings, but they may just have cold hands. Another example is lack of eye contact. For some cultures, this is a sign of respect for authority; therefore, interpreting it as sadness may be inaccurate. Crisis workers should remember that nonverbal cues are just one piece of information that helps assess clients' affective reaction to a crisis. All information must be used, forming a gestalt, in order to accurately assess clients' affective reaction.

Obviously, crisis workers using hotlines cannot rely on their vision to identify nonverbal behaviors. Instead, they must utilize hearing and questions to assess nonverbal behaviors when talking with clients via telephones, listening for background noises and asking questions to verify interpretations. Footsteps, for example, indicate that a client may be pacing, which in turn suggests that a client is either angry or anxious. Crisis workers should test their interpretation of the footsteps by reflecting the feeling back to the client: "You seem anxious," or "You seem angry." Panting may indicate anxiety. The sound of sniffing may indicate sadness. By listening to background sounds, crisis workers can, by continually verifying the meaning of those sounds, be attentive to nonverbal behaviors even though they are talking on the telephone. Another problem with telephone contact is how to interpret silence. Silence on the telephone is more ambiguous than when one is working with clients in person (Milman, Strike, Van Soest, Rosen, & Schmidt, 1998). When silence occurs, crisis workers must ask clients what is happening. Direct questions, such as "What is happening with you right now?" or statements such as "You got quiet after talking about . . . ," can be used to help clients verbalize the meaning of the silence and express their feelings.

Using Voice Quality

Voice quality also provides crisis workers with clues to assess clients' affective reaction. Citing results from research conducted on speech patterns when people were angry, anxious, or sad, Siegman (1993) indicated that volume and rate of speech correlates with specific affect. In each case, researchers found that speech patterns differ for a person who is in a heightened state of emotional arousal. For a person who is angry, speech patterns involve shorter pauses and increased volume and rate of speech. A person who is anxious tends to use an accelerated rate of speech, a higher pitched voice, and fewer long pauses. In addition, Siegman cited research indicating that an anxious person's responses are longer than when not in a state of anxiety. Finally, a sad person utilizes a slow rate of speech and talks softly. These general findings can be useful for crisis workers as they determine clients' affective reactions to a crisis.

Using Questions

Along with observing nonverbal behaviors and being attentive to voice quality, gathering the information needed to assess clients' affective reaction also includes the use of questions and statements. Combined, this information is sufficient for crisis workers to accurately assess affective reactions to a crisis. Crisis workers can focus questions and clarifying statements on salient information. This concentration, in turn, helps clients recognize their feelings. Since by definition, a crisis occurs when clients' resources are overwhelmed, they may not be cognizant of their feelings, or they may minimize or rationalize them. Asking questions that help clients recognize their feelings is therefore therapeutic. Clarifying statements, which permit crisis workers to further hone in on clients' affective reactions, have a similar function. Crisis workers use clients' comments, being attentive to nonverbal behavior and voice quality, to formulate statements such as "You appear to be feeling . . ." or "I get the idea you are . . ." Clients will generally confirm the statement or correct it, saying something like, "No, I feel more like . . ." The important thing is for crisis workers to help clients identify their reactions. This recognition facilitates clients' resolution of the crisis.

Beginning and inexperienced crisis workers may have difficulty identifying clients' affective reactions because clients do not always report being angry, anxious, or sad. Instead, clients may say they are frustrated as opposed to being angry, jittery rather than anxious, or lonely instead of sad. Table 3.2 contains a partial list of words that clients may use to report their emotions. These emotions

TABLE 3.2 COMMONLY USED AFFECTIVE WORDS

Anger/Hostility	Anxiety/Fear	Sadness/Melancholy
Outraged	Panicked	Depressed
Furious	Terrified	Hopeless
Annoyed	Scared	Crushed
Irritated	Overwhelmed	Miserable
Mad	Worried	Defeated
Enraged	Frightened	Dejected
Exasperated	Jittery	Unhappy
Aggravated	Tense	Lonely
Frustrated	Shaky	Hurt
Upset	Jumpy	Down
Hostile	Nervous	Discouraged
Pissed off	Stressed	Disappointed
Insulted	Uptight	Blue
Incensed	Anxious	Left out
Violated	Afraid	Dismal
	Fear	Pathetic

represent varying degrees of the affect under which they are listed. Notice that this list includes colloquialisms. For example, a client might say "I feel left out" to express feelings of sadness/melancholy or "I'm pissed off because of what happened" to express anger/hostility. Being familiar with this list helps crisis workers accurately identify clients' affective reaction. Remember also that colloquialisms and phrases will vary according to geographic region, as well as ethnic background. In these situations, clients may use languages other than English to express their feelings. Crisis workers are urged to become familiar with phrases common to the area in which they live as well as the ethnic groups with which they work.

Guidelines for Assessing Affect

The following guidelines are suggestions as crisis workers assess clients' affective reactions. Utilization of these suggestions can make the assessment process flow evenly and help to establish rapport with clients.

1. For angry clients, crisis workers need to acknowledge the anger, but also set firm limits with respect to clients acting out their anger (Kleespies et al., 1998). Limits should include behaviors that might result in injury to others or to themselves (e.g., hitting a wall or banging their head).

2. Never touch clients that are angry. If clients' primary affective reaction to a crisis is anger, crisis workers should stay at least one arm's length away.

3. Straightforward questions are more effective for angry clients (Dubin, 1990). These questions help prevent clients from believing that crisis workers are attempting to deceive or trap them. Direct, concrete questions help angry clients feel empowered.

4. For clients whose primary affective reaction is anxiety, crisis workers should be more structured in the interview process (Cormier & Cormier, 1998). The structure can help decrease the anxiety, thereby increasing the amount of information that can be gathered.

5. For anxious clients, reassurance that they are in a protective, supportive environment will facilitate expression of feelings (Kleespies et al., 1998).

6. For clients who react with sadness as the dominant feeling, crisis workers must be patient and supportive. Often these clients will need time and empathy to tell their story.

ASSESSMENT OF SEVERITY

Simply knowing clients' affective reactions is not enough to understand what and how to intervene. Crisis workers must also gauge the severity of the affective reaction. They must also keep in mind that culture influences how affective reactions are expressed (Herrera, 1996), a variable that makes assessment of severity challenging. Regardless of the primary affective reaction, its expression will vary by culture. For example, most cultures allow for an emotional expression of affect during funerals, but after that, customs vary about how people are to behave. African Americans, for example, may be expressive in their emotions as they grieve (Perry, 1993), while Jewish people may be more reserved and focused on expressing respect for the person who has died (Cytron, 1993). Many cultures discourage the outward expression of emotion, especially in the presence of people who are not family members (Egli et al., 1991). Crisis workers must be aware of this tendency and adjust assessment methods appropriately. Being cognizant of cultural diversity when assessing the severity of clients' affective reaction is critical to accurate assessment.

Over- or underestimating the severity may result in clients believing they have not been helped. If crisis workers overestimate clients' affective reaction, clients may feel as if crisis workers have not listened to them and only want to tell them what to do. If crisis workers underestimate the severity of the affective reaction, clients may also feel that they were not helped. For suicidal or homicidal clients, in particular, the consequences of underestimation could be disastrous. Therefore, accurate assessment of the severity of clients' affective reaction is crucial. Crisis workers have two primary methods to assess the severity of client's affective reactions: (a) observation and clients' self-report and (b) the report of others associated with clients.

Observation

Nonverbal Indicators Alertness to such things as clothing, personal hygiene, posture, and motor activity provides useful information for assessing the severity of the affective reaction. Crisis workers working on hotlines can use questions to obtain this information. These questions should be asked in a matter-of-fact manner and be structured to obtain information that helps crisis workers understand the general demeanor of clients. Questions concerning appearance, bathing, appetite, sleeping patterns, and level of activity since the crisis all help crisis workers understand the severity of clients' reaction to the crisis. For example, to obtain information about a client's personal hygiene, a crisis worker might ask a female client if she has done anything for herself lately, like polish her nails or fix her hair; a male client might be asked about shaving. Clients might also be asked if they regularly exercise and if that has changed. This information, while seemingly not related, does provide crisis workers with valuable information regarding the severity of clients' affective reaction.

First impressions can be misleading and may have to be adjusted as the assessment proceeds. For example, in the case described at the beginning of the chapter, Sandy arrived with her hair uncombed and wearing wrinkled clothing with splashes of food on it. This appearance might suggest a severe affective re-action. However, a few minutes into the interview, Sandy revealed that she taught at a day-care center, helping to serve lunch and watch the children while they played outside. With this information, the crisis worker should look for other evidence to help determine the level of severity and possibly modify the initial assessment.

With respect to clothing, crisis workers should observe its appropriateness and neatness. Is the client's clothing disheveled or too neat? For example, a client arriving at an interview in a professionally cleaned suit the day after sur-viving a natural disaster such as an earthquake appears unusual. Asking a ques-tion about this can help crisis workers understand the intensity of the emo-tional reaction to the crisis. The client may say that there was nothing else to wear since the rest of his or her clothing was destroyed. This may simply tell a crisis worker the degree of loss experienced by the client. However, a client may say something to the effect that he or she had to dress this way since every-thing else was in shambles. This response may suggest a coping mechanism, but it also signals a possible acute emotional reaction.

Personal hygiene refers to maintaining a culturally and situationally appro-priate level of personal cleanliness. Awareness of clients' personal hygiene in-volves a sensitivity to cultural issues and socioeconomic status. Not all cultures or socioeconomic groups maintain the same standard of personal hygiene as middle-class Euro-Americans. Yet, using an ordinary standard that can be ad-justed according to circumstance, crisis workers can use personal hygiene to as-sess the severity of clients' affective reaction to a crisis; the greater the depar-ture from the norm, the more severe the affective reaction.

In terms of posture and motor activity, crisis workers should be attentive to possible fidgeting, marked quiescence, avoidance of eye contact, an ex-tremely fast or slow gait, and inability to remain seated. Is the client slumping? This might indicate sadness. Is the client walking and sitting rigidly? This might indicate anger. Any behavior observed immediately, either in the field or in an agency, is useful to determine the severity of the affective reaction to a crisis.

Verbal Indicators   Clients' tone of voice—volume, rate of speech, and voice inflection—can also provide clues regarding the severity of their affective re-action. Generally, the more voice tone deviates from customary speech pat-terns, the more intense the affective reaction. Shouting or very quiet speech, for example, may indicate greater severity. Speaking either very fast or slow also provides valuable information for appraising the severity of clients' feelings. Halting speech is another indicator. For example, clients who find it difficult to control an angry reaction may clench their teeth, resulting in halting speech patterns. Speech may also be halting if clients are sad. Voice inflection is another indicator of affective reaction. For example, clients may be monotone when talking with crisis workers. Their feelings may be so intense that they have closed them off in order to cope with the crisis. Or, inflection may be so varied that clients sound like they are singing, suggesting that clients are unable to close off their feelings.

Report of Others

In addition, the severity of clients' affective reaction can be assessed through the report of family or friends (Kleespies et al., 1998). There may be times, as a result of the crisis, when clients are unable to speak for themselves. In these instances, crisis workers must rely on information from family or friends, who can provide information on previous level of functioning, fill in missing information, and give other relevant data such as medical history and compliance with medication (Kleespies et al., 1998). At other times, crisis workers may need to rely on police, firefighters, or paramedics to provide information. Often in these circumstances, clients will require either hospitalization or an extended session in order to recover enough to be capable of functioning. Crisis workers should be alert in these incidents to any exaggeration by these people. In a few situations, the person giving the information may either over- or underestimate clients' reactions. For example, in possible abuse situations, family members may not be accurate in their reporting (Kemp, 1998). Therefore, when interviewing family or friends, crisis workers should try to verify the information if possible.

Assigning Severity Rating

By combining the different kinds of information obtained, crisis workers can assess the severity of clients' affective reaction using the Affective Severity Scale on the Triage Assessment Form (see Appendix B). The Affective Severity Scale is divided into six categories ranging from "No Impairment" to "Severe Impairment." Table 3.3 lists each category, summarizing the characteristics used to rate clients. Note that each category also contains rating values. The anchor categories—No Impairment and Severe Impairment—each have one rating value, while the remaining four categories have two rating values. The purpose for the two rating values is to allow crisis workers to assess clients as being low or high in those categories.

Begin with the Severe Impairment category, or a rating value of 10; this allows you to move down the list until you believe the client's affective reaction matches at least one of the descriptors in that category. If the client's affective reaction falls between 2 and 9, select the lower or higher value in that category. In general, clients matching a majority of the descriptors in a particular category should be given the higher value; otherwise, they should be rated with the

TABLE
3.3

AFFECTIVE SEVERITY SCALE COMPONENTS

Rating Value	Category	Descriptors	Characteristics
1	No Impairment	Stable mood with normal variation of affect appropriate to daily functioning.	Client recognizes and readily identifies emotions associated with crisis. Routine day-to-day activity not affected by affective reaction to crisis.
2 & 3	Minimal Impairment	Affect appropriate to the situation. Brief periods during which negative mood is experienced slightly more intensely than situation warrants. Emotions are substantially under client control.	Client's affective reaction to the crisis does not interfere with day-to-day emotional expression. Client may express moodiness and irritability, but is able to control this when desired. When asked, client is able to regulate emotional expression associated with crisis.
4 & 5	Low Impairment	Affect appropriate to situation but increasingly longer periods during which negative mood is experienced slightly more than situation warrants. Client perceives emotions as being substantially under control.	Client's affective reaction appears expected given the situation. Client recognizes moodiness is associated with crisis. Clients state that if busy they are able to forget about the crisis. Yet, if reminded of the crisis or idle they begin reexperiencing the crisis.
6 & 7	Moderate Impairment	Affect may be incongruent with situation. Extended periods of intense negative moods. Mood is experienced noticeably more intensely than situation warrants. Lability of affect may be present. Effort required to control emotions.	Client expresses concern over not feeling normal. Affective reaction to crisis predominates all emotional expression. A typical variation of emotional expression not present in day-to-day activities. Given the situation, client is noticeably unable to regulate mood and expresses a sense of being overwhelmed. Client reports emotions seem to be cycling and a feeling of being out of control. Client reports effort is required to express emotions other than those associated with crisis. If presented with competing stimuli, unable to maintain control of emotions.
8 & 9	Marked Impairment	Negative affect experienced at markedly higher level than situations warrants. Affect may be obviously incongruent with situation. Mood swings, if occurring, are pronounced. Onset of negative moods are perceived by client as not being under volitional control.	Client expresses affect openly without discretion or forethought. Affective reaction to crisis becomes associated with events other than crisis. Client's affective reaction is excessive given the situation. At times, clients believe they are "crazy." Clients recognize their incapacity to control mood and are concerned with being viewed as "crazy."
10	Severe Impairment	Decompensation or depersonalization evident.	Client may be in shock, be unable to talk, and appear catatonic. Client unable to express any emotion. Client may be hysterical and unable to regulate affective expression.

lower value. At times, clients may match fewer than half the descriptors, but should be given the higher value because their reactions are so intense that the higher rating value is justified. For example, consider the case of John, a client with suicidal ideations. John is a student in high school who typically did well academically. He went to the school counselor one afternoon after receiving a poor grade on an English paper. During the interview, the counselor discovered that John's parents held high expectations of him, demanding that he do well. John stated that his parents wanted him to major in journalism and attend the best school in the nation for that subject. John had not told his parents of the grade and was becoming increasingly unable to control his anxiety. After about a week of feeling this way, John made the contact with the counselor to figure out what to do. He stated that sleeping was becoming increasingly difficult and that during the past two nights he had slept very little. Within the first 10 minutes of the interview, the counselor asked John if he had thoughts of killing himself. John answered yes, stating that just last night he had gone to the bathroom looking for the prescription pain medication he had been taking for a sprained ankle two months earlier. He reported that the medication bottle was not there, but that he would have taken the medication if he had found it. John stated that his anxiety had increased that morning as he thought about what he had almost done. Although John matched only two of the five descriptors found in the Moderate Impairment category, the counselor assessed the value as 7. The two descriptors that matched John's affective reaction to receiving a poor grade were "affect may be incongruent with the situation" and "effort required to control emotions." In the counselor's judgment, John did not match the two descriptors concerning mood disturbance because the period of time, one week, was short. Neither did the counselor observe lability (i.e., frequent, quick changes) of affect. However, because John's feelings of anxiety appeared so powerful that they were causing him to consider suicide as an option, the counselor believed a rating of 7 was warranted. Crisis workers must rely on clinical judgment gained through experience and training to handle such situations.

One of the key factors that distinguishes the categories is duration; note, for example, that negative mood is experienced for "brief periods" in the Minimal Impairment category and for "increasingly longer periods" in the Low Impairment category. When does the experience of a mood change from brief to increasingly longer periods? Crisis workers must judge the overall impact of the crisis on clients' day-to-day functioning. Clients experiencing "brief" negative moods generally are able to maintain their daily routine, whereas clients experiencing "increasingly longer periods" of negative moods are not. They find they must keep increasingly busy or they will think about the crisis.

Another problem encountered by crisis workers when assessing the degree of clients' affective reaction involves the intensity of feelings or moods. For example, the descriptors "incongruent" and "obviously incongruent" can be found in the Moderate Impairment and Marked Impairment categories, respectively. Again, experience and clinical judgment are needed. In John's case, for example, is his affective reaction simply "incongruent," or is his reaction pronounced enough to be "obviously incongruent" with the situation? The crisis worker had to listen attentively to how John talked about his feelings. John recognized that his reaction to the low grade was not normal, and was aware that his anxiety was extreme. He was frightened by his suicidal ideas, and realized that he needed help. These factors suggested to the counselor that although John was aware of his feelings, he was experiencing incongruent affect. This awareness, as well as his apparent control over how and when he would disclose his feelings, led the counselor to assess John's affective reaction in the Moderate Impairment category as opposed to the Marked Impairment category.

Finally, when rating clients on the Affective Severity Scale, crisis workers should err on the side of being slightly conservative because the potential consequences of a rating that is too low—lack of treatment—are worse than those of a rating that is too high. Crisis workers should also avoid dramatically inflating clients' affective reaction—for example, an assessment of 8 (Marked Impairment) that should have been a 5 (Low Impairment). Such inflation also puts crisis workers at risk for malpractice charges. Crisis workers must provide a responsible level of intervention; failure to do so, either through neglect or error, can lead to malpractice suits (Bednar, Bednar, Lambert, & Waite, 1991). Generally, however, assessments that are one to two values too high will not result in difficulties.

SUMMARY

Remember that no two clients react the same in a crisis. Some clients may display extreme emotion to a minor incident; others may exhibit an almost undetectable affective reaction to a significant crisis. In addition, people react differently to different crises. Just because a client reacts with anger in one crisis does not mean that he or she will react with anger in another crisis. Crisis workers must use their knowledge of human behavior, sensitivity to cultural norms, and their clinical experience to make sound judgments. Further, crisis workers must assess how congruent the reaction is with the crisis event. Assessment is based on clients' reaction, but it is not divorced from the context of the event. Consider a person having a minor car accident, a "fender bender." Some emotional reaction is expected. A person might get angry or be anxious. The person might express the reaction by shouting and possibly other verbal abuse. However, if this person begins threatening physical harm or reacts by threatening huge lawsuits, the reaction would be considered excessive. Crisis workers must, therefore, consider the context of the reaction.

Affective reactions to crisis events are often obvious; sometimes, however, the emotional reaction is complex and unclear. Crisis workers must utilize their experience and training when sifting through the information as they assess this aspect of clients' reactions. Further, they must be on the lookout for different kinds of information. Clients will present with nonverbal cues such as physiological responses, gestures, and tone of voice. Crisis workers also must factor in clients' cultural heritage. All this information merges to form a gestalt that provides an accurate picture of clients' emotional reaction to a crisis. By treating each situation and each client individually, crisis workers will be able to accurately assess clients' affective reaction.

POINTS TO REMEMBER

- Expression of emotion is healthy for people in crisis. Clients should be allowed to express their feelings provided these are not harmful to themselves or others.
- Crisis workers should "share the pain" or empathize with clients in order to establish rapport, while still maintaining the professional distance necessary to ensure effective intervention.
- Crisis workers must be aware of their own emotions to ensure accurate assessment of clients' affective reaction, especially if they have experienced a similar crisis.
- Primary emotions (anger/hostility, anxiety/fear, sadness/melancholy) are affective reactions to crises.
- Differentiation of affect and mood is critical when one is assessing clients' affective reactions.
- Both verbal and nonverbal behaviors are indicators of clients' affective reactions and the severity of the reaction.
- Voice quality is also an indicator of clients' affective reaction. Things such as rate of speech, volume, and pitch all can be used in the assessment of affective reactions.
- If the client cannot communicate, crisis workers may need to use reports from family and friends in the assessment of affective reactions and the severity of the reaction.
- In the Affective Severity Scale, clients' affective reactions are assessed on a scale from 1 (No Impairment) to 10 (Severe Impairment).
- When using the Affective Severity Scale, crisis workers should start from the Severe Impairment category, stopping when at least one of the descriptors fits. If more than half of the descriptors fit, the higher rating of that category should usually be assigned.

STUDY QUESTIONS

1. The case of Sandy found at the beginning of the chapter describes her interview with a crisis worker. What information described in the case is useful for assessing Sandy's affective reaction to learning that she may have cancer? Does your assessment of her affective reaction change depending on what you believe the crisis to be?
2. What colloquialisms or phrases, other than those listed in Table 3.2, might clients use to express their feelings?
3. How would you assess the affective reaction of the case example of the family whose mother just died? What information would you use? After the initial emotional outburst, what would you suspect to happen with respect to the severity level?
4. How are affective reactions of Sandy and the family whose mother died (see pages 37–38) alike or different? On what do you base your response?

REFERENCES

Akiskal, H. S., & Akiskal, K. (1994). Mental status examination: The art of the clinical interview. In M. Hersen & S. M. Turner (Eds.), *Diagnostic interviewing* (2nd ed., pp. 21–51). New York: Plenum.

American Counseling Association. (1995). *Ethical standards of the American Counseling Association.* Alexandria, VA: Author.

American Psychological Association. (1992). *Ethical principles of psychologists.* Washington, DC: Author.

Baldwin, B. A. (1979). Crisis intervention: An overview of theory and practice. *Counseling Psychologist, 8*(2), 43–52.

Bednar, B. L., Bednar, S. C., Lambert, M. J., & Waite, D. R. (1991). *Psychotherapy with high-risk clients.* Pacific Grove, CA: Brooks/Cole.

Birdwhistell, R. L. (1970). *Kinesics and context.* Philadelphia: University of Philadelphia Press.

Bloom, B. L. (1984). *Community mental health* (2nd ed.). Monterey, CA: Brooks/Cole.

Caplan, G. (1964). *Principles of preventive psychiatry.* New York: Basic Books.

Cormier, W. H., & Cormier, L. S. (1998). *Interviewing strategies for helpers: Fundamental skills and cognitive behavioral interventions* (4th ed.). Monterey, CA: Brooks/Cole.

Crow, G. A. (1977). *Crisis intervention.* New York: Association Press.

Cytron, B. D. (1993). To honor the dead and comfort the mourners: Traditions from Judaism. In D. P. Irish, K. F. Lundquist, & V. J. Nelsen (Eds.), *Ethnic variations in dying, death, and grief: Diversity in universality* (pp. 113–124). Washington, DC: Taylor & Francis.

Dixon, S. L. (1979). *Working with people in crisis: Theory and practice.* St. Louis: Mosby.

Dubin, W. R. (1990). Psychiatric emergencies: Recognition and management. In A. Stoudemire (Ed.), *Clinical psychiatry for medical students* (pp. 497–526). Philadelphia: J. B. Lippincott.

Eddy, S., & Harris, E. (1998). Risk management with the violent patient. In P. M. Klees-pies (Ed.), *Emergencies in mental health: Evaluation and management* (pp. 217–234). New York: Guilford.

Egli, E. A., Shiota, N. K., Ben-Porath, Y. S., & Butcher, J. N. (1991). Psychological inter-ventions. In U. S. Department of Health and Human Services (Ed.), *Mental health services for refugees* (pp. 157–188). Rockville, MD: National Institutes of Mental Health.

Greenstone, J. L., & Leviton, S. C. (1993). *Elements of crisis intervention: Crises and how to respond to them.* Pacific Grove, CA: Brooks/Cole.

Hackney, H., & Cormier, S. (1994). *Counseling strategies and interventions* (4th ed.). Bos-ton: Allyn & Bacon.

Herrera, R. (1996). Crisis intervention: An essential component of culturally competent clinical case management. In P. Manoleas (Ed.), *The cross-cultural practice of clinical case management in mental health* (pp. 99–118). New York: Haworth.

Hoff, L. A. (1995). *People in crisis: Understanding and helping* (4th ed.). San Francisco: Jossey-Bass.

James, R. K., & Gilliland, B. E. (2001). *Crisis intervention strategies* (4th ed.). Pacific Grove, CA: Brooks/Cole.

Kanel, K. (1999). *A guide to crisis intervention.* Pacific Grove, CA: Brooks/Cole.

Kemp, A. (1998). *Abuse in the family: An introduction.* Pacific Grove: CA: Brooks/Cole.

Kennedy, E. (1981). *Crisis counseling.* New York: Continuum.

Kleespies, P. M., Deleppo, J. D., Mori, D. L., & Niles, B. L. (1998). The emergency inter-view. In P. M. Kleespies (Ed.), *Emergencies in mental health practice: Evaluation and management* (pp. 41–72). New York: Guilford.

Lindemann, E. (1944). Symptomatology and management of acute grief. *American Jour-nal of Psychiatry, 101,* 141–148.

Lindemann, E. (1956). The meaning of crisis in individual and family living. *The Teachers College Record, 57,* 310–315.

Milman, J., Strike, D. M., Van Soest, M., Rosen, N., & Schmidt, E. (1998). *Talking with the caller: Guidelines for crisisline and other volunteer counselors.* Thousand Oaks, CA: Sage.

National Advisory Mental Health Council. (1995). Basic behavioral science research for mental health. *American Psychologist, 50,* 838–845.

Ouellette, R. (1993). *Management of aggressive behavior.* Powers Lake, WI: Performance Dimensions.

Perry, H. L. (1993). Mourning and funeral customs of African Americans. In D. P. Irish, K. F. Lundquist, & V. J. Nelsen (Eds.), *Ethnic variations in dying, death, and grief: diversity in universality* (pp. 51–66). Washington, DC: Taylor & Francis.

Plutchick, R. (1980). *Emotion: A psychoevolutionary synthesis.* New York: Harper & Row.

Roberts, A. R. (1996). Epidemiology and definitions of acute crisis in American society. In A. R. Roberts (Ed.), *Crisis management and brief treatment* (pp. 16–34). Chicago: Nelson-Hall.

Schwartz, M. F. (1997, April). *Post traumatic stress disorder.* Keynote address at Crisis Convening XXI, Chicago.

Siegman, A. W. (1993). Paraverbal correlates of stress: Implications for stress identification and management. In L. Goldberger & S. Breznitz (Eds.), *Handbook of stress: Theo-retical and clinical aspects* (2nd ed., pp. 274–299). New York: Free Press.

Sue, D. W., & Sue, D. (1999). *Counseling the culturally different: Theory and practice* (3rd ed.). New York: Wiley.

CHAPTER

ASSESSMENT OF COGNITIVE REACTIONS

4

Mr. Jonathan Everett is a 43-year-old white male who has been married for 21 years. His family consists of his wife, a daughter 16, and a son 12. He called the crisis center for an appointment and insisted it be the first appointment the next day. In the telephone call, Mr. Everett said there was a family problem that he must take care of immediately. Although asked to explain more on the telephone, Mr. Everett said the problem was too important to be settled on the telephone. An appointment was made and he arrived 10 minutes early. Mr. Everett was dressed in a business suit and carried a briefcase. When asked to come into the office, he walked in quickly and sat in the chair facing the door. Mr. Everett began his story by apologizing for his call the day before and his insistence on being the first client. He added that he hoped he had not inconvenienced the crisis worker. At that point, he launched into his story. Mr. Everett said that two nights ago his daughter had announced she was pregnant. Mr. Everett reported that he was shocked since he and the girl's mother had taken her to church every Sunday. He added that he was even an elder in the church. As he continued, Mr. Everett said he was worried about what others would say; after all, it was a small town where everyone eventually finds these things out. Mr. Everett reported having difficulty sleeping over the past two nights, saying he could not stop thinking about this problem and wondering what he would say when people came into his business. He worried about whether they knew, whether they would be polite and not say anything, whether they would judge him in some negative way, whether they would continue to do business with him, and so on.

The case of Mr. Jonathan Everett illustrates the difficulty in assessing clients' cognitive reaction to a crisis. Before clients' cognitive reaction can be assessed, crisis workers must know what the client sees as the crisis. In this case example, is the crisis the fact his daughter is pregnant? Is it possibly feeling he failed as a parent? Is it this client's seeming embarrassment or his business suffering because of the pregnancy? Is it his concerns about his position in the church? Mr. Everett may believe his station as an elder is in jeopardy. Any one or combination of these may be the crisis for Mr. Everett. The issue is that in order to accurately assess Mr. Everett's cognitive reaction, the crisis worker must determine the nature of the crisis.

Accurate assessment of clients' cognitive reactions is especially important because of the potential for long-term effects. Too often, crisis workers do not recognize the importance of precise assessment in this area. They tend to focus on affective and behavioral reactions, which are relatively easy to observe and assess. Once clients' emotional reactions have subsided and their behavior resembles normal day-to-day functioning, the belief is that the crisis has ended. However, crisis workers also need to attend to clients' cognitive reactions. Failure to do so can result in psychological or mental health problems surfacing years after the crisis event (Meichenbaum & Fitzpatrick, 1993).

This chapter describes strategies crisis workers can utilize in assessing clients' cognitive reactions. First, I will outline the crisis workers' role in the assessment process. The key issue to understand is that crisis workers must view the crisis using clients' perception of the event. How does the client see the event? Second, I explain the three types of cognitive reactions: transgression, threat, and loss. Third, I will discuss the four life dimensions introduced in Chapter 2—physical, psychological, social, and moral/spiritual—in relation to crisis intervention. Fourth, I will explain the assessment of clients' cognitive reaction on the Cognitive Severity Scale of the Triage Assessment Form (see Appendix B), offering practical suggestions for accurately assessing clients' cognitive reaction to a crisis.

CRISIS WORKERS' ROLE

Assessing clients' cognitive reaction to a crisis can be troublesome for crisis workers. Too often, crisis workers have difficulty distinguishing their perceptions from clients' perceptions of the crisis. Take, for example, the case of Mr. Everett. Does he perceive the crisis as embarrassment and losing business along with his standing in the community? If so, assessment of his cognition reaction would focus on threat to his social relationships. Or, does Mr. Everett believe that he has failed as a parent? If so, the crisis worker would focus on his psychological well-being as well as a loss of his relationship with his daughter. Intervention for these two possible cognitive reactions would be quite different. If the crisis worker misunderstands the father's cognitive reaction, he or she will not be in a position to help him. Crisis workers must be cautious when assessing clients' cognitive reactions, taking care to listen to the client closely and to avoid imposing their own view of the situation.

Importance of Using Clients' Perception

Crisis workers must strive to perceive the crisis as if they were the client. This requires recognition and appreciation of clients' culture, because cultural elements shape the way people view the world (Herrera, 1996). For example, Euro-Americans tend to view crises in terms of cause and effect, while some Asian and Native American cultures might appeal to folk or supernatural explanations to interpret crisis events (Sue & Sue, 1999). Consider the development of nightmares following a traumatic event. Euro-American culture would likely ascribe the cause of the nightmares as the crisis event; that is, the client is having nightmares because the crisis is unresolved. A client from some Asian cultures might perceive the cause of the nightmares very differently, believing that spirits are causing the nightmares. The point is that people from different cultures tend to perceive events according to what they learned from their culture. Taking this factor into consideration is, therefore, necessary to make accurate assessments.

Assessment of cognitive reactions is, in a sense, double edged. Crisis workers must be able to see the crisis through the eyes of the client. At the same time, however, because a crisis by definition overwhelms resources and coping mechanisms—including perception—the meaning clients attach to an event may ignore or misconstrue information, and thus crisis workers must sometimes help clients to interpret the situation (Meichenbaum & Fitzpatrick, 1993). But what is perception? According to Ormrod (1999), because we are flooded with information from all our senses (i.e., smell, sight, hearing, taste, and touch), we must be able to attend to relevant information and ignore irrelevant information to construct an overall understanding of the environment. Schunk (1996) labels this process *pattern recognition*—the ability to attach meaning to the information received through our senses. In crisis situations, clients perceive the environment (the crisis event) and attempt to attach meaning to the event on the basis of their ability to recognize a pattern. However, their ability to recognize a meaningful pattern may be impaired. At this point, crisis workers must be able to see what the client sees, even if it seems wrong. If the client appears to be experiencing perceptual overload, the crisis worker must help the client achieve a more realistic orientation.

Problems Associated with Accurate Assessment

Crisis workers often experience problems in four areas. First, crisis workers may minimize or discount clients' perception. Minimizing generally occurs for one of two reasons. First, crisis workers engage in this behavior in order to manage their feelings of inadequacy and powerlessness to help clients (Yassen & Harvey, 1998). This situation is not unusual in crisis intervention. By definition, clients present with overwhelming needs and are generally passionate about asking for help. Crisis workers must learn to balance their desire to help with the reality of their ability to help, which may be limited by any number of factors (e.g., agency constraints, skill, and time). Yet, learning to live within those limitations is crucial if crisis workers are to be effective. Second, when crisis workers believe the crisis event is not significant enough to merit a crisis, they may believe clients' reactions are not appropriate. Instead, crisis workers may feel clients are simply catastrophizing over a relatively minor incident. This situation arises when crisis workers become cynical. For example, in the case study at the beginning of the chapter, the crisis worker might downplay or even dismiss Mr. Everett's experience of crisis, simply referring him to an abortion clinic in a neighboring city. This situation typically occurs when crisis workers become cynical and rely on "pat" responses to resolve crises. Crisis workers fail to listen, resulting in a faulty assessment of clients' cognitive reaction.

Second, crisis workers may impose their own cognitive reaction on the client. This situation may take place when crisis workers have experienced similar crises in their lives that they have not fully resolved. Instead of being attentive to clients' perception, crisis workers glide through the assessment process presuming they know how clients are perceiving the crisis. This lack of attentiveness imposes a preconceived cognitive reaction on the situation that results in incorrect assessment and premature solutions. James and Gilliland (2001) address this issue by debunking the myth that crisis workers must have "lived in the crisis" in order to be helpful. While having experienced a similar crisis is helpful, this is not necessary to do crisis intervention. Personal experience must be balanced with training in order to accurately assess cognitive reactions.

Third, crisis workers may use former clients or parallel cases to judge clients' cognitive reaction. Here, again, crisis workers are not attentive to the uniqueness of each client's perceptions. Instead of listening, crisis workers become impatient, believing they have heard this story before. Crisis workers simply want to get through the process and provide a stock answer rather than tailoring the intervention to a particular client's needs. Hoff (1995) cautions against this practice, stating that perception of the event is one of the factors that differentiates people's reactions to crisis. By jumping to conclusions, crisis workers implement erroneous interventions that can be harmful. The danger is that this damage may not be seen for several years. Clients who do not fully resolve a crisis are prone to develop psychological or mental health problems after the incident (Meichenbaum & Fitzpatrick, 1993).

Fourth, crisis workers may use individual counseling theories rather than crisis theories to assess clients. This is especially important with respect to clients' cognitive reactions to a crisis. While an overlap exists, assessment of clients in crisis cannot rely on individual counseling theories. Take Rational Emotive Behavioral Therapy, for example. Two focal tenets of this theory of counseling posit that people can stand "noxious" events and that events are hardly "awful" (Ellis, 1995). For individual counseling, these tenets are appropriate and helpful for clients to overcome irrational beliefs. For crisis intervention, however, these tenets are inappropriate and cause crisis workers to inaccurately assess clients' cognitive reactions.

In assessing clients' cognitive reactions, crisis workers must put aside assumptions and preconceived ideas about how people are supposed to react. Not doing so leads to the erroneous assessment of clients' cognitive reaction, and thus inadequate interventions. Crisis workers must remember that a key element in the definition of a crisis is that it is in the "eye of the beholder." That is, a crisis takes place in the perception of the person experiencing the event and believing it is a crisis. Using this concept as a fundamental principle when assessing clients' cognitive reactions helps crisis workers avoid flawed assessments.

COGNITIVE REACTIONS

Assessment of clients' cognitive reactions to a crisis is often neglected by crisis workers. Instead, crisis workers tend to focus on affective and behavioral reactions, believing these to be more salient to the intervention process. When clients are able to control their emotions and return to a daily routine similar to precrisis functioning, the reasoning goes, the crisis is then over. This initial recovery, according to experts in the field, takes approximately 6 weeks (Callahan, 1998). Callahan, however, believes that after 6 weeks a person has simply achieved a restored sense of stability and has not fully resolved the crisis. Similarly, Haan (1993) believes people who have experienced a crisis may adopt a false, rigid stability in response to prolonged and unremitting stress. Consequently, unless crisis workers develop interventions targeting clients' cognitive reactions, the potential exists that clients will settle into a chronic state that represents lower functioning than their precrisis functioning level (Callahan, 1998). The development of interventions addressing clients' cognitive reactions is, therefore, solely dependent on crisis workers' ability to assess these reactions accurately (Janosik, 1984).

Threat and Loss

A pioneer in understanding cognitive reactions to crises is Rapoport (1962, 1965). Clients' reactions to hazardous situations, she argues, may result in them believing they are vulnerable or in conflict and unable to cope. The reactions, according to Rapoport (1965), are dictated by clients' perception or cognitive interpretation of the situation and fall into two categories: "threat" and "loss." For her, threat signifies the reaction clients experience when fundamental, instinctual needs or a person's integrity is jeopardized. Loss, on the other hand, means clients experience either an actual loss or may be in a state of "acute deprivation" (p. 25). However, looking at threat and loss in this manner may be limiting. Clients can perceive a threat or a loss in ways other than described by Rapoport. For example, clients can perceive a threat to personal relationships, occupational goals, emotional well-being, and so on. Loss also may be perceived as chronic, not just actual or acute. In spite of these constraints, Rapoport's work gave direction to examining clients' cognitive reactions to crises.

Results from Lazarus and Folkman's (1984) research on stress bear a striking resemblance to Rapoport's work (1965). In their book, *Stress, Appraisal, and Coping,* the researchers introduce the "cognitive appraisal model of stress." This model focuses on the process used to interpret the meaning of the event, a key element of which is people's judgment about what is at stake; the more at stake, the more potential for a situation to be perceived as stressful. As this research progressed throughout the 1980s, Folkman et al. (1991) found that in order for a situation to be stressful, people must perceive or appraise it as either a "threat" or "loss" that affects them in a personal way. That is, whatever a person believes is at stake (e.g., health, personal relationships, financial security, or occupational status), they must perceive a threat or loss in order to experience stress.

Since the introduction of the appraisal model, these authors, along with others (e.g., Gall & Evans, 1988; Stanton, Tennen, Affleck, & Mendola, 1991), have written extensively in this area. Threat, according to the model, involves clients perceiving the potential for harm or occurs when there is an uncertainty about the outcome of a situation (Folkman et al., 1991). For example, waiting for the results of a medical test may induce a perception of threat. The person does not know what to expect and therefore perceives the situation as threatening. In this research, loss refers to damage or harm already done. The definition of loss in this literature is much broader than Rapoport's (1962, 1965). In addition to the actual loss of an object, this literature also includes the perception of injury or harm already done. Such perceptions would seem to be distinct, but they are not (Folkman et al., 1991). For example, while a divorce may be seen as a loss of a relationship, it may also be perceived as a threat to financial security. The reason they cannot be considered distinct is because different aspects of a person's life are affected by a situation (Folkman et al., 1991).

Transgression

Research examining the perception of threat and loss establishes a firm foundation for explaining clients' cognitive reactions to crises. Yet, this research falls short in accounting for the range of cognitive reactions. The perception of a threat relates to the future, while the perception of loss relates to the past. Absent is a cognitive reaction or perception that relates to the present. Transgression occurs when people perceive that their rights are currently being violated (Ellis & Harper, 1975; see also Slaikeu, 1990). That is, someone or something is behaving in a manner that violates the personal standards of a person or socially accepted guidelines.

Again, the literature on stress adds to the understanding of transgression as a type of cognitive reaction to a crisis. Lazarus (1993) examines the experience of a "demeaning offense against me and mine" (p. 26). Such offenses occur when core relational issues are violated and a person's self-esteem is at stake. The result is stress. The violated person may attribute blame to another person if it is believed that the person could have acted otherwise (Lazarus, 1993). The case at the beginning of the chapter is a good example. Mr. Everett may perceive his daughter's behavior as a demeaning offense to himself—a transgression—blaming her and believing she could have acted otherwise; his daughter acted thoughtlessly, resulting in his self-esteem being jeopardized. The importance of understanding the different aspects of a person's life that are affected by the situation is again evident (Folkman et al., 1991). Mr. Everett's perception of himself as a good parent is being challenged, and his position in the church and his reputation in the community are also being compromised.

LIFE DIMENSIONS

Unlike affective and behavioral reactions, cognitive reactions must be assessed in relation to clients' lives. Simply assessing if clients perceive a transgression, threat, and/or loss is inadequate in planning accurate interventions. Rosenfeld (1984) states that crisis assessment must include a component identifying the areas of a client's life that are affected. Crisis workers must know what clients believe is at stake to formulate interventions that will help resolve the crisis. Although this area is often neglected in the assessment process (Hoff, 1995), most experts in the field of crisis intervention agree that it is important. Hoff, for example, states that crisis workers risk misidentifying who is in crisis and the exact nature of the crisis unless they consider the sociocultural context of the crisis. Aguilera (1994) echoes this belief, stating that crisis workers must identify the segment or segments of clients' lives affected by a crisis in order to understand the meaning clients impose on crisis situations.

The Triage Assessment Form identifies four life dimensions to be used in assessment of crisis situations. Table 4.1 defines and gives examples of the life dimensions: (a) physical; (b) psychological; (c) social relationships; and (d) moral/spiritual. These categories parallel Maslow's (1970) hierarchy of needs, according to which people must satisfy basic needs prior to fulfilling needs higher in the hierarchy. For example, before fulfilling esteem needs, a person must be assured that needs related to physiological functioning, safety, and belonging are met. Similarly, life dimensions are viewed as hierarchical in that clients must begin by addressing issues related to the physical domain prior to resolving issues involving the other domains. Once these issues are met, clients can move

TABLE 4.1 DEFINITION OF LIFE DIMENSIONS	
Life Dimension	**Definition**
Physical	Aspects of a person's life involving physical safety and comfort (e.g., food, water, shelter, financial security)
Psychological	Aspects of a person's life involving intrapersonal elements (e.g., self-concept, emotional well-being, personal identity, self-esteem, self-efficacy)
Social Relationships	Aspects of a person's life involving relationships including family, friends, co-workers
Moral/Spiritual	Aspects of a person's life that involve issues related to integrity, belief systems, values, moral convictions, religious beliefs

to the psychological well-being domain. After addressing the issues related to this domain, clients are able to direct their attention to the social relationship domain. Finally, after satisfying concerns in these domains, clients are able to work on issues pertaining to the moral/spiritual domain. Although theoretically the intervention process is intended to follow this model, in practice the model breaks down after the first step, resolving issues related to the physical domain. Experts (e.g., Bongar et al., 1998; James & Gilliland, 2001; Hoff, 1994; Kemp, 1998; Roberts, 1996; Weaver, 1995; Yassen & Harvey, 1998) in the field agree that meeting physical needs is paramount in crisis intervention. Ignoring these needs may lead to disastrous results such as suicide and homicide. However, after ensuring that issues in the physical domain are satisfied, crisis workers should address concerns in the remaining domains in the manner that is suitable for that client and situation.

Although research directly examining the life dimensions aspect of crisis intervention is lacking, research on stress is relevant. Examining the relationship of events that may cause stress to the way the events are perceived, Lazarus and Folkman (1984) found that stress responses are mediated by people's appraisal of the stressor: The more potential for harm or danger people perceive, the greater the stress response. According to these researchers, a key element in the appraisal process is people's commitments, which serve as a reference point in evaluating stressors. If a stressor is perceived as hazardous to commitments, people experience stress.

Similarly, Emmons (1986) concluded that people experience stress to the degree that the attainment of personal goals is frustrated or jeopardized. Other researchers have found similar results, according to Browning (1996). In an innovative study of his own, Browning examined personal goals as a means of predicting stress responses. Although Browning fell short of his goal of prediction, data from this research suggested that personal goals are related to stress responses.

In summary, this literature supports the need to assess clients' cognitive reactions with respect to affected life dimensions. This information helps crisis workers understand the significance of the crisis for clients, and without it, crisis workers cannot devise interventions tailored to individual clients. For example, an intervention for a young pregnant woman whose moral/spiritual life dimension is primarily affected would be different from an intervention for a young pregnant woman whose physical life dimension is primarily affected. The intervention for the moral/spiritual life dimension might include a referral to a minister, priest, or rabbi, while an intervention for the physical life dimension might involve a referral to a medical clinic. The same young woman might need either or both.

ASSESSMENT OF COGNITIVE REACTIONS

Generally, clients are less able to communicate their cognitive reactions than their affective reactions (Morley, Messick, & Aguilera, 1967). The confusion and surprise that accompany most crises may contribute to clients' inability to verbalize cognitive reactions. Further, crises are most often associated with emotional reactions and, therefore, clients may not attend to or believe that their cognitive reactions are as serious. Or, clients may confuse cognitive reactions with either emotional and/or behavioral responses. They may not be able to differentiate cognitive reactions from other, seemingly more salient, reactions. Still another contributing factor may be that crisis workers are not as attuned to assessing cognitive reactions, choosing to focus on either affective or behavioral reactions. If not asked, clients may ignore or gloss over cognitive reactions because they are following crisis workers' leads. Yet, assessment of cognitive reactions is critical in determining interventions that lead to long-term healthy postcrisis adjustment. Failure to assess cognitive reactions may be life threatening.

Cognitive Indicators of Suicidal and/or Homicidal Ideations

A word of caution is essential: Crisis workers must always be alert for situations in which clients' cognitive reactions may lead to suicide or harm to another person. The consequences of failing to recognize cognitive reactions of this nature expose crisis workers to legal and ethical charges made by clients and their families (Bednar, Bednar, Lambert, & Waite, 1991). Clients whose cognitive reaction to the crisis is transgression are potentially violent. Since this reaction involves clients perceiving someone or something is victimizing them, clients may believe the way to resolve the crisis is to retaliate. This desire for revenge can lead clients to direct physical attacks on whatever or whoever they believe caused the crisis. Newspapers and television news programs regularly report incidents such as this. Clients perceiving a threat may also choose to respond with aggression toward others. Again, clients may believe the only way to end the threat is to strike back. Often clients will feel justified in these situations and be quite surprised if they are legally charged with some type of wrongdoing. However, clients experiencing a crisis as a threat may also embrace suicide as an option in order to end their suffering. In this situation, clients may believe the only way to stop the crisis is to end their lives. They believe the only hope to end the pain is to do it permanently. When clients perceive a loss, crisis workers should also be alert for suicidal ideations. A key characteristic in determining lethality for clients with suicidal ideations is recent losses (James & Gilliland, 2001). Without exception, crisis workers should assess for suicidal ideations when clients have experienced a significant loss within the recent past. Please keep in mind that not all clients are suicidal or homicidal. A simple guideline is, the more severe the reaction, the more unable clients are to distinguish between socially acceptable and unacceptable courses of action. More will be said about determining when crisis workers should ask about suicidal and/or homicidal thoughts in the section on assessing severity.

Obstacles in Assessing Cognitive Reactions

As noted, clients may be unable to report cognitive reactions precisely because they may be too overwhelmed and not able to identify the areas of their lives that are impacted. Clients may be in shock, omitting vital information, because they are unable to remember it, or they may report the information out of sequence (Kennedy, 1981). This situation occurs when clients experience an especially catastrophic crisis, including such things as sexual assault (Myer, Ottens, & Uden, 1994), violent crime (Pynoos, Sorenson, & Steinberg, 1993; Yassen & Harvey, 1998), natural disasters (Weaver, 1995), acute illness or critical injuries (Myer & Hanna, 1996), and terrorist situations like being held hostage (James & Gilliland, 2001; Ofman, Mastria, & Steinberg, 1995). In these circumstances, crisis workers must exercise patience in the assessment process. Forcing the assessment process may cause clients to engage in resistant behaviors. Clients always need to feel a sense of support (Kennedy, 1981), and not be hurried to disclose information they are unable or may be unwilling to report (Yassen & Harvey, 1998). General questions such as "Tell me what happened?" and "What does this mean for you?" may not illicit coherent or usable responses. Instead, crisis workers should ask questions that are direct and call for specific information, such as "When did this take place?" and "Who else have you told about this?" Clients may be calmed by this type of question and find such questions easier to answer.

An example of a situation involving a client being overwhelmed by a crisis and unable to respond to general questions occurred several years ago while I was working in a hospital emergency room. The crisis involved a husband and wife who were visiting the city. On the first evening in town while leaving a restaurant, the husband experienced chest pains. Within minutes he lay on the sidewalk with a nurse who just happened to be passing by performing CPR on him. Unfortunately, this valiant effort was not enough and the man was pronounced "dead-on-arrival" at the hospital emergency room. Although the emergency room staff was able to get basic medical information from the woman, they were unable to coax her into providing anything else. I was asked to speak with the woman in order to gather information that would facilitate obtaining the necessary information regarding funeral arrangements, assistance for herself, and dealing psychologically with the death of her husband. During the interview, the woman was unable to initiate any conversation, but responded to questions when asked. Although cooperative in responding, she would respond to questions asking for general information with "I don't know" or "I can't think right now." Therefore, I began patiently asking very specific questions to attain the information needed to close the case. For example, I asked if she knew anyone who lived in the city, to which she answered "no." I then asked if she had a family member who lived in the city, to which she answered "yes." This example illustrates that when in a crisis state, clients may find it difficult or impossible to remember simple information. Crisis workers must maintain their composure and be diligent in assessing clients' cognitive reactions.

Another problem crisis workers face in assessing clients' cognitive reactions is clients who are unable to talk about anything other than their feelings or the actual event. This type of reaction is not unusual, yet it irritates crisis workers. Knowing the information is needed, crisis workers may resort to confrontational, unproductive methods. While confrontation is not without its use in crisis intervention, these strategies should only be used with caution during the assessment process. Crisis workers may also resort to trying to calm and/or cheer clients too quickly. Statements such as "This is normal" or "Look at the silver lining" do not communicate that crisis workers understand; rather, such platitudes indicate that crisis workers are unable, uncomfortable, or unwilling to listen to clients. In order to assess clients' cognitive reactions, crisis workers need to communicate a willingness to listen to clients as they tell their story. Interruptions or abrupt clichés are not effective in the assessment process.

Again, patience by crisis workers is essential in gathering the needed information. One strategy that is useful when clients persist in talking only about feelings or the crisis event is validation. When clients' experience and feelings are validated, they realize someone is listening to them and understanding their devastation. This technique works almost as if by magic in most situations. However, do not be fooled into believing that clients only need to be validated once. Crisis workers may need to validate clients repeatedly in the assessment process. Remember, clients are overwhelmed and unable to concentrate. In fact, they may be in psychological shock due to the crisis and therefore not able to focus their thoughts (Golan, 1978). Validation generally takes the form of identifying and reflecting back to clients their emotion. Examples of statements

that can be used to validate clients are: "You seem . . ."; "I get the idea you are . . .";
"I sense you feel . . ."; "So, from where you are sitting . . ." By filling in the blanks
with appropriate statements, crisis workers validate clients' experiences. As
stated previously, crisis workers must take care in not lapsing into the use of
clichés, which can be annoying and result in clients feeling that they have not
been helped.

Another way crisis workers can gather information on clients' cognitive reactions is to interview family members, friends, and/or others who have knowledge of the crisis. However, care must be exercised if others are used in the assessment process. Crisis workers must take into consideration two guidelines.
First, crisis workers must bear in mind the stake others have in the crisis situation. Do they have reasons for misleading the assessment process? For example,
in the case of child abuse, a parent may report that the child has simply fallen
or is just at a clumsy stage. The same idea is relevant for elderly abuse, which
is a growing problem. Second, crisis workers must evaluate the effect of the crisis event on the person providing the information. Did the crisis affect him or
her? If so, how much? Was that person also involved in the crisis, and if so, to
what degree? More often than not, if a family member is providing the information, the crisis has affected him or her in some way. To make an accurate assessment, crisis workers must take this knowledge into consideration. Other people
can provide valuable information during the assessment process, but crisis
workers must remember these two guidelines to prevent incorrect assessments.

A final impediment to assessing clients' cognitive reactions is the interview
process itself (Perlmutter & Jones, 1985). If clients are not familiar with being
interviewed and asked questions, they may perceive the interview process as
threatening, which may cause them difficulty in recalling information and responding to questions. As the interview progresses, clients may become increasingly hesitant to disclose personal information, giving curt responses and
becoming resistant to expanding their answers. Inexperienced crisis workers
may become impatient, falling into an interview style that resembles cross-
examination rather than an empathetic attempt to understand clients' reactions.
When this type of situation occurs, one of three things has happened. First, crisis workers are expecting clients' reactions to match how they would react, in a
sense, imposing their values on clients. For example, a client may express a transgression reaction because her spouse has just been diagnosed with Alzheimer's
disease. Crisis workers might expect this client to experience a threat or a loss,
not a transgression. Unless careful, crisis workers might impose their values at
these times by leading the client to believe she should be experiencing a threat
or loss. A second problem related to the interview process for assessing cognitive reactions occurs if clients believe that they, family members, and friends
may be at risk of legal problems. For example, clients tend not to be forthcom-
ing with information in crises involving domestic violence (Kemp, 1998). If
clients believe disclosure on their part may result in a family member or friend

becoming the subject of legal difficulties, they may not provide accurate information, thereby hindering the assessment of their cognitive reactions. Third, sometimes crisis workers attempt to change the subject and talk about other things. For example, I was involved in talking with a family who had just been told their father was terminal and not expected to live through the night. Their minister happened to arrive a few minutes after the family received this sad news. During the first few minutes, while the family shared this information with their minister, they cried and were noticeably distraught. Surprisingly, after hearing about the father's condition, the minister began talking about the renovations at the church and how lovely the sanctuary would be. After the minister departed, the family expressed dismay that they had not been asked anything about their reactions at being told their father was going to die within the next few days.

Avoiding these obstacles is impossible, yet being aware of them helps crisis workers sidestep them in most instances. The challenge is knowing if and when the assessment process is being compromised. A safe assumption is to presume that the assessment process inevitably is complicated by clients' inability to fully communicate their reactions (Perlmutter & Jones, 1985). Although the use of dependable assessment strategies helps to minimize mistakes, some degree of error is likely because of the inability to obtain complete, accurate information from clients. For example, after a natural disaster a client may not be able to report accurately about where he or she was when the disaster occurred. A few hours, or possibly a few days, may pass before the client is able to remember his or her location during the crisis. Therefore, crisis assessment is invariably ongoing in order to continually amend and correct inaccurate information.

Clients' Time Orientation and Cognitive Reactions

Attending to the client's time orientation may yield useful information about his or her primary cognitive reaction: Does the client seem to be oriented toward the past (loss), the present (transgression), or the future (threat)? This information consistently provides a window to understand clients' perception of the crisis and facilitates the development of interventions. As with the other elements of assessment, culture plays an important role in clients' perception of time. Some cultures, for example, emphasize the future while others may focus on the past, the present, or a combination of the three. For Asian Americans, time orientation is primarily past and present (Sue & Sue, 1999), and crisis events are likely to be interpreted within this orientation. For Native Americans, the time orientation is more present oriented, according to Sue and Sue, meaning that this group may tend to perceive crisis events as affecting the present more than the past or future. This is not to say that individuals from these cultures are limited only using these time frames. Rather, knowledge of these time

TABLE 4.2	COGNITIVE REACTIONS IN RELATION TO TIME ORIENTATION

Cognitive Reaction	Time Frame	Typical Client Statements
Transgression	Present	"No one should have to take that." "I am not going to let that happen." "Why is this happening to . . .?" "Why doesn't he or she just stop?"
Threat	Future	"I don't know what will happen to . . ." "I am not sure I can take any more . . ." "How can I bear this any longer?" "What should I do?" "Where can I find help?"
Loss	Past	"If only I had . . ." "I wonder what would have . . ." "I feel cheated because . . . is missing." "My life hasn't been the same since . . ." "Nothing will ever be as good as . . ." "I really miss . . ."

orientations may assist crisis workers to be more culture sensitive. Table 4.2 identifies the associated time frame for the three types of cognitive reactions and provides typical statements clients might use to indicate their perception of the crisis.

As Table 4.2 indicates, talking about the crisis as something in the present indicates that clients are experiencing a transgression. Statements made by clients with this cognitive reaction may sound like a demand or pleading. The perception is that something has happened that is an infringement on their rights and that some aspect of their life has been victimized. If clients talk about the crisis as something in the future, the crisis is perceived as a "threat." Clients may communicate a sense of anticipation, vulnerability, and/or the experience of being confused. Clients experiencing this cognitive reaction may appear emotionally needy and defenseless. Finally, talking about the crisis as something in the past indicates that a client is perceiving a loss. Note that clients' statements are of two types. In the first type, clients fantasize about not having an experience because something has been taken away. Two examples of something clients might say are "I'll never get to see my son/daughter get married" and "No one could ever want to be with me now that I have been raped." Although on the surface these statements seem to be future oriented, in fact clients making these statements are perceiving a loss. That is, they are imagining what their life would be like if something or someone were present rather than missing. The second type of statement is more straightforward. An example is a client who says, "I'll miss my friend." In these types of statements, clients express a longing for an object or someone. It is obvious that these clients' cognitive reaction is that of loss and that they are experiencing grief.

Several research studies suggest that eye movement and position express whether clients are thinking of the past, present, or future (Cormier & Cormier, 1998). Although the reliability of this research is questionable, crisis workers can use this type of information in combination with other information. Cormier and Cormier suggest that looking up indicates a future orientation, looking down suggests a past orientation, and looking straight ahead means a person is thinking about the present. Crisis workers can use this as an adjunct to confirm clients' cognitive reactions. For example, a client who is looking up and yet talking about his or her reaction as if it were in the present may be giving misleading information. Crisis workers may also use eye movement and position to help guide the assessment process. This is particularly useful when clients are hesitant to disclose information. Crisis workers can observe eye movement and position, using this to form a question to determine clients' cognitive reactions. For example, if a client is looking down, the crisis worker might ask, "What are you remembering?" If the client's eyes consistently move up, a crisis worker might say, "You seem to be thinking about what is going to happen." Again, eye movement and position is not sufficient to determine clients' cognitive reactions. The research on this topic is not conclusive, so caution must be exercised in interpreting eye movement. However, knowing this material can provide a starting point for crisis workers and help them ask appropriate questions to insure the assessment is correct.

Crisis workers should *not* use clients' affective reaction as a guide. Even though literature on stress suggests that specific affective responses are paired with certain cognitive reactions (e.g., transgression/anger, threat/anxiety or fear, loss/sadness; Folkman et al., 1991; Lazarus, 1993; Lazarus & Folkman, 1984), cognitive reactions in crisis situations do not seem to be paired with affective reactions in this way. For example, I have observed clients who have perceived a situation as a threat respond with each of the three affective reactions: anger/hostility; anxiety/fear; and sadness/melancholy. Likewise, I have also observed clients whose cognitive reactions are transgression and loss react with all three affective reactions. Therefore, using clients' affective reaction to assess cognitive reactions is not advisable since there is no consistent relationship. The explanation for this phenomenon may lie in the life dimension that is affected by the crisis.

ASSESSMENT OF LIFE DIMENSIONS

Cognitive reactions are complex, usually involving several areas of clients' lives. Clients may talk about the past with respect to one life dimension, and in the next sentence switch to discussing the same issue as affecting the future in another area of their lives. This situation can be confusing and intimidating for crisis workers as they try to understand clients' perceptions. The harder crisis workers try to understand, the more confused they may become. Crisis workers must keep in mind the reality that clients are in crisis; that is, they are overwhelmed and not able to logically process the impact of the crisis. Expecting clients to rationally and coherently tell their story should not be expected. Ordinarily, the closer in time the assessment takes place to the crisis event, the more likely clients are to be uncertain of their cognitive reactions and the life dimensions that are affected. The further away in time the assessment takes place from the crisis event, the more likely clients will be able to identify their perceptions and the life dimensions that are affected. Remembering this simple axiom can prevent needless annoyance for crisis workers. Crisis workers can also avoid becoming unduly aggravated in the assessment process by monitoring their reactions to clients. Becoming impatient and wondering why clients cannot stay on one topic or just say what they mean are two signs that crisis workers have not understood what is being said. This situation may occur when crisis workers are distracted by the detail rather than examining the larger context of the crisis. A strategy to overcome this problem is to take a proverbial step back to examine the overall picture of clients' stories.

Since crisis workers are assessing life dimensions according to the perception of clients, culture should have minimal effect on the assessment. Yet, two issues merit discussion. First, as noted, crisis workers must be careful not to impose their perceptions on clients. Being able to distinguish your perception from a client's is an essential skill in this area of crisis assessment—and particularly needed when providing services for clients who are from a culture different from one's own. Assessing a client's reaction on the basis of the crisis worker's perception can lead to ineffective and possibly harmful interventions. Therefore, in the assessment of life dimensions affected by a crisis, sensitivity to cultural values is important. Second, crisis workers should recognize that some cultures put more, or less, emphasis on the four life dimensions. For example, Latin and Asian Americans might place more emphasis on family relationships than Euro-Americans.

Because verbal information is the primary vehicle for assessing the life dimensions that are affected by a crisis, the process is similar for crisis workers talking in person or on the telephone. Generally, crisis workers will not have to ask clients to talk about the life dimensions that are affected. This content is ordinarily communicated during the course of the assessment process. As clients talk about the crisis and the impact it is having on their lives, they will disclose how this has, is, or will affect various parts of their lives. Crisis workers should listen for this information, matching it with the four life dimensions: physical, psychological, personal relationships, and moral/spiritual. Remember that clients will not say, "My psychological well-being is threatened" or "My moral/spiritual belief system is lost." Instead they may say, "I'm crazy," or "I think I will never be the same." Crisis workers must learn to discern the meaning of clients' statements to make accurate assessments.

Repeated content is extremely important in the assessment process. The more often clients discuss a specific life dimension, the more distress they are experiencing in that domain. Remember that different content may refer to the same life dimension. The case study involving Mr. Everett is a good example of this point. As you recall, Mr. Everett's 16-year-old daughter recently told him she was pregnant. Mr. Everett became distraught and sought professional help. In this case, although Mr. Everett mentions three life dimensions (i.e., psychological, personal relationships, and moral/spiritual) that have been affected, one is mentioned significantly more often. The life dimension that is repeated throughout the case is "personal relationships." He discusses this using several contexts. The first is when he talks about taking his children to church. The next time Mr. Everett talks about his personal relationships is when he mentions being an elder of the church. A third time he discusses this issue is when he talks about what everyone in the town will think. And a fourth instance comes as Mr. Everett wonders specifically about his business and customers. The crisis worker in this case assessed Mr. Everett's primary cognitive reaction as a threat to personal relationships.

While clients readily discuss the life dimensions affected by a crisis, open-ended probing questions also can be used to help crisis workers gather additional information. This facilitates the assessment process in two ways. First, it ensures that clients are not leaving out relevant information. Again, because clients are in a state of disequilibrium, they may not think to disclose relevant information. While listening to clients discuss their reactions, crisis workers must listen not only to what is said, but also what is left out. By listening to what is not talked about, crisis workers can form questions that will explore those areas. It is possible that clients have not experienced any reaction in that area, but confirmation of that is needed if the assessment is to be accurate. Again, consider the case of Mr. Everett. Although he stated that he had a family problem, he came alone to see the crisis worker. The crisis worker might ask about that and the reaction of the remainder of the family to the pregnancy. If Mr. Everett said nothing about other changes in his life, such as appetite or use of alcohol, the crisis worker might ask about these to help understand how much the crisis has intruded on his day-to-day life. Using their experience, crisis workers can speculate on what may be happening with clients and ask questions that will explore those areas. Second, if clients are resistant to being deflected from discussing a specific life dimension as questions are asked, it is likely the crisis has a greater impact on that area. For example, clients repeatedly returning to discuss a topic after responding to other questions indicates that that life dimension has been affected to a greater degree than the others. If Mr. Everett persists in talking about his business and how his customers will react, it is likely this is what he perceives as the most significant issue of the crisis. This information helps crisis workers determine intervention strategies to address the problem associated with that life dimension.

A final note on life dimensions. Crisis workers must guard against being sidetracked into "psychological archeological digs" that lead to doing "personal counseling" rather than crisis intervention (Bloom, 1984). A common phenomenon in crisis intervention is the uncovering of information that is fertile ground for more long-term, personal counseling approaches (Okun, 1982). Many times this information is uncovered as crisis workers assess the impact of the crisis on clients' life dimensions. For example, in a domestic violence situation a crisis worker may discover that the client was sexually abused as a child or came from a very dysfunctional family. In this case, the crisis worker should focus on resolving the domestic violence issue and not venture into working out issues related to the sexual abuse or dysfunctions of the family of origin. If addressed, these issues should only be discussed in relationship to the crisis at hand. Referral to another counselor is preferred for clients to resolve issues related to these problems.

ASSESSMENT OF SEVERITY

Knowing clients' cognitive reactions and the life dimension that is affected by a crisis helps crisis workers target their intervention efforts. However, crisis workers must also evaluate the severity of clients' reactions in order to determine if this area should be addressed first and how direct the intervention process should be. Crisis workers must be as accurate as possible in this phase of the assessment process in order to avert psychological problems that may emerge in the future as well as to prevent destructive efforts to resolve the crisis in the present. Therefore, careful attention should be given to this segment of the assessment process. Several methods can be used to assess clients' cognitive reactions.

Thought Form

First, crisis workers should observe clients' ability to relate their stories in a logical, cogent fashion. Akiskal and Akiskal (1994) refer to this ability as clients' "thought form." This method does not rely on questions asked by crisis workers as much as a clinical judgment about the general manner in which clients put together thoughts and ideas. Crisis workers should watch for coherent thought that is clear and forms a pattern that can be followed. The clearer the thought and more consistent the pattern, the less severe the reaction. Particular attention should be given to problems such as clients using too much detail to tell their story, changing subjects in mid-sentence, a fixation with one thought or concept, and an inability to recall information. At times, clients may insist on explaining every detail no matter how small or subtle. This situation generally occurs when the crisis is so overwhelming that clients focus on details in order to avoid the overall brunt of the crisis. Crisis workers must exercise patience with clients who tell their story in this way and not pressure clients unduly. Clients who feel inordinately pushed may become hesitant to disclose information due to feeling a lack of empathy from the crisis worker. However, not pushing clients at all is not productive. Crisis workers must find the balance between tolerating clients' pace and the use of probing questions that moves the assessment process along. One method to interrupt clients who are absorbed in minutiae is to become more structured in the assessment process. Crisis workers may interject, saying that some specific information is needed in order to get the most appropriate type of help. If this method is used, crisis workers should be prepared with a series of questions that will gather the needed information. These questions may come from a set of standard questions that are designed to encourage clients to discuss their cognitive reactions or may be composed on the spot and tailored to the specific situation.

Clients may also seem to stop in the middle of a sentence and then resume talking on an entirely different topic. Sensitivity to this can help crisis workers by alerting them that important information has been camouflaged or censored altogether. Crisis workers may want to ask clients about what just happened when this situation occurs. Examples of questions that can refer clients back to the missing information are: (a) "Just a moment ago you seemed to be thinking about something; what was that?" (b) "I have a hunch that you were thinking about something important when you stopped in the middle of what you were saying; were you?" (c) "What happened when you were quiet just a second ago?" Other questions may also be used, but these suggestions are examples of non-threatening questions that ordinarily are effective. Typically, the more often clients don't finish sentences and change the subject, the more severe the cognitive reaction. Another clue crisis workers can use to assess the severity of clients' cognitive reaction involves fixation on one aspect of the crisis; clients will become preoccupied with one aspect of the crisis regardless of its relative importance. For example, instead of talking about and/or minimizing the personal trauma and life-threatening injuries in the aftermath of a tragic automobile accident, a client only wants to describe the damage done to the car. In this situation, the client's cognitive reaction, whether it be transgression, threat, or loss, is so intense that the client is able to discuss only aspects of the crisis that are less painful. When this situation occurs, crisis workers must be sensitive to what information is left out or avoided in addition to what information is disclosed. Creating a safe, supportive environment for clients to feel secure enough to discuss this material is therefore critical. Crisis workers can accomplish the creation of a reassuring environment by validating the trauma of clients' experience. Simple comments such as "That sounds painful" or "You seem really paralyzed as you talk" will work wonders in building rapport. Inability to recall information is also a hallmark of severe cognitive reactions to a crisis. In this situation, clients may be unable to recall basic information such as their phone number, address, family members' names, their age, and so on. As noted, direct questions asking for specific information are needed. Clients whose cognitive reaction is this severe are unable to access information when asked general questions but are much better at responding to questions asking for specific information. Crisis workers may also have to rely on others to fill in missing information for clients who are not able to remember this information. In addition, it is important to remember that clients may have the information in their purses or wallets.

Thought Content

Second, the thought content (Akiskal & Akiskal, 1994) or clients' self-report and reports from others may be used to estimate the severity of the cognitive reaction. This information can be gathered in two ways. First, crisis workers can simply observe, listen, and make inferences from the content of clients' stories. For example, clients may talk about being forgetful since the crisis; they may experience difficulty remembering lock combinations or passwords to access e-mail and other computer-linked activities. Clients may also complain of not being able to follow recipe directions or complete tasks involving a series of steps such as programming a VCR to tape a program. Listening for these types of problems helps crisis workers gauge the severity of clients' cognitive reactions. The more clients complain of these problems, the more severe the cognitive reaction. Crisis workers should also be attentive to clients' personal hygiene and general ability to maintain activities needed for day-to-day living. Simply noticing the level of grooming, asking about the last time clients ate or bathed, communicates a great deal about the severity of their reaction to the crisis. The less able clients are in maintaining the socially accepted standards needed for day-to-day functioning, the more severe the cognitive reaction. Second, crisis workers can ask direct questions regarding clients' preoccupation with the crisis and ability to concentrate to determine the severity of clients' cognitive reactions. Questions should cover the four life dimensions and assess whether clients are experiencing a transgression, threat, and/or loss in the domains affected by the crisis.

Assigning Severity Rating

The Cognitive Severity Scale of the Triage Assessment Form can be used as a means to gather and synthesize the information described above (see Appendix B). The Cognitive Severity Scale is similar to the Affective Severity Scale. Both are divided into six categories ranging from "No Impairment" to "Severe Impairment," with each category consisting of rating values. And, as with the Affective Severity Scale, the anchor categories have one rating value while the middle four have two rating values each. Table 4.3 lists each category and summarizes the characteristics used to rate clients.

TABLE
4.3

COGNITIVE SEVERITY SCALE CATEGORIES

Rating Value	Category	Descriptors	Characteristics
1	No Impairment	Concentration intact. Client displays normal problem-solving and decision-making abilities. Client's perception and interpretation of crisis event match with reality of situation.	Client able to recall personal information with no effort. Client capable of following verbal directions to be carried out immediately or in the future. Client performs tasks needed for daily functioning with no effort. Client will not accept directives from crisis worker.
2 & 3	Minimal Impairment	Client's thoughts may drift to crisis event but focus of thoughts is under volitional control. Problem-solving and decision-making abilities minimally affected. Client's perception and interpretation of event substantially match with reality of situation.	Client able to recall personal information, but may experience difficulty with information not often used (e.g., phone numbers of friends and extended family members). Client capable of remembering verbal directions to be carried out immediately but has difficulty if these are not written when carried out later. Client able to accomplish tasks needed for daily living but may put these off for a limited time. Client may request directives from crisis worker, but will consider these as suggestions.
4 & 5	Low Impairment	Occasional disturbance of concentration. Client perceives diminished control over thoughts of crisis event. Client experiences recurrent difficulties with problem-solving and decision-making abilities. Client's perception and interpretation of crisis event may differ in some respects with reality of situation.	Client able to recall personal information when asked. Client capable of following verbal directions to be carried out immediately but has difficulty remembering these for more than a few minutes. Client recognizes the need to perform tasks needed for daily living but may postpone performing these because of being preoccupied with the crisis event. Client accepts directives from crisis worker as suggestions and uses these as springboard to develop others.

6 & 7	Moderate Impairment	Frequent disturbance of concentration. Intrusive thoughts of crisis event with limited control. Problem-solving and decision-making abilities adversely affected by obsessiveness, self-doubt, confusion. Client's perception and interpretation of crisis event may differ noticeably with reality of situation.	Client able to recall personal information that is used daily (e.g., address, phone number, names of immediate family), but other information (e.g., names of extended family and friends, work phone numbers) will not be recalled. Client capable of following directions provided these are to be carried out immediately. If the directions are to be used later, these must be written. Client tasks needed for daily functioning with effort. Client embraces directives from crisis workers as guidance in resolving the crisis.
8 & 9	Marked Impairment	Client plagued by intrusiveness of thoughts of crisis event. The appropriateness of clients' problem-solving and decision-making abilities likely adversely affected by obsessiveness, self-doubt, confusion. Client's perception and interpretation of crisis event may differ substantially with reality of situation.	Client able to recall personal information with prompting. Client capable of following directions only if these are not complicated (one or two commands). Client may forget or neglect some tasks needed for daily living because of being distracted by crisis event. Client accepts willingly directives from crisis worker.
10	Severe Impairment	Client so afflicted by obsessiveness, self-doubt, confusion that problem-solving and decision-making abilities have "shut down." Client's perception of crisis event may differ substantially from reality of situation as to constitute threat to client's welfare.	Client unable to recall personal information (e.g., phone number, address, names of family members, age, birth date, etc.). Client incapable of following simple directions. Client unable to perform routine tasks needed for daily living such maintaining personal hygiene. Client willingly accepts directives from crisis worker and performs these without question.

As with assessing affective reactions, the most effective way to begin assessing clients' cognitive reactions is to start at the highest category and go down. When a client matches at least one of the descriptors in a category, that is the category in which he or she should be assessed. Notice that descriptors in several categories require crisis workers to make clinical judgments that concern clients' interpretation of the event as opposed to reality. Care must be taken to guard against imposing crisis workers' values at these times. Instead, assessment should focus on identifying clients' perceptions about whether they should or could have prevented the crisis and/or should or could deal with the situation without help—regardless of what the crisis worker may know about the situation.

The two rating values for the four middle categories are particularly helpful for crisis workers trying to decide between two categories, which can be difficult, particularly for crisis workers with limited experience and for other human service workers who do not regularly do crisis intervention. The standard rule is: If clients exhibit more than half of the descriptors in a category, they should be assigned the higher value; if less than half, they should be assigned the lower value. Consider Mario, a client fitting into the Low Impairment category. If Mario reports thinking about the crisis several times a day and wants to talk about it, but stops himself because he knows that not everyone is interested in hearing the story over and over, he probably should be assigned a value of 4. If Mario also reports that he is experiencing difficulty thinking about anything but the crisis and states that the quality of personal decisions made since the crisis has suffered, the crisis worker should assign a value of 5. However, as with the affective scale, there are times when even though clients may fit fewer than half of the descriptors in a particular category, they should still be assigned the higher value. To make this judgment, crisis workers must also consider the intensity of clients' cognitive reaction. If Mario reports that he has been able to keep from talking about the crisis but has avoided people in order not to bore others with the problem, the crisis worker might consider assessing the cognitive reaction as a 5 rather than a 4. Because clients are not likely to use the exact words found in the descriptors in Table 4.3, crisis workers must listen carefully to make the judgment to determine what value should be given to a specific client's reaction. Crisis workers will need to look beyond the content and instead listen for how the crisis is affecting clients' capacity to function.

The column labeled "Characteristics" in Table 4.3 gives specific examples of functioning for each of the descriptors and categories. Listed are four characteristics that most people have no difficulty performing. First, can the client recall personal information such as address, often-used telephone numbers, names of family members, and names of several friends? If in crisis, he or she may not be able to access this information. People are not able to concentrate and recall what appears to be simple information. Thoughts of the crisis seem to short-circuit clients' capacity to remember this information. The more severe the cognitive reaction, the less people are able to recall this type of information. Crisis workers can either directly ask clients to provide it or infer it from what they say during the interview process. The less able clients are to answer questions, the more severe the reaction. However, remember that specific questions must be asked. For example, if a crisis worker wants the address of a client and asks, "Where do you live?" clients may say "I don't know," "in a house," "in Pittsburgh," or something similar. The question "What is your address?" would more likely elicit the information if the client is able to recall it. Crisis workers can also use inferences. During the assessment interview, clients may indicate they have had trouble remembering things. By listening to how often and how pervasive this problem is, crisis workers should be able to infer the clients' cognitive reaction.

Second, can the client follow directions involving two or more steps? The more clients have problems following directions, the more severe the cognitive reaction. As they describe what their lives have been like since the crisis, listen for complaints that everything is too complicated or that they are not able to read directions anymore. The client who prior to the crisis used the mass transit system in a city now may complain of confusion and being overwhelmed, not able to understand how to get around. The client who complains of not being able to remember how to use his or her computer or other electronic equipment since the crisis event is another example. Or, a client may complain of difficulty following cooking recipes that used to be easy. Simply listening to the description of clients' day-to-day activities provides valuable clues to their cognitive reactions. Third, can the client perform the tasks necessary for daily functioning? The more clients report they are having problems with or not eating, sleeping, bathing, interacting with others, and/or maintaining a satisfactory work schedule, the more severe the cognitive reaction. Crisis workers may choose to ask questions regarding these functions, but most often these issues will emerge naturally during the assessment process. Fourth, is the client willing to accept directives from crisis workers? The more acquiescent clients are, the more severe the reaction. Assessment of this characteristic can be accomplished by simply asking clients to do something. Crisis workers may suggest that clients contact someone regarding the crisis or do something that will help resolve the crisis. The more willing clients are to follow through on these suggestions, the more severe the reaction.

Summary

Accurate assessment of clients' cognitive reactions to crises is critical in the prevention of future psychological problems. Too often, crisis workers neglect and even ignore this aspect of clients' reactions. Crisis workers are most likely to attend to affective and behavioral reactions because these are generally the most easily identified. Once clients have calmed down and are able to control their emotions, it is as if the crisis is over. In truth, however, it is at this juncture that the full resolution of the crisis begins. Attending to clients' cognitive reactions is essential in the development of holistic interventions.

Each client's perception of a crisis is unique. Everyone will react on the basis of culture, experience, and immediately available resources. Recognizing this fact is crucial in the assessment of cognitive reactions. Also, remember that different family members will perceive a crisis differently. A classic example involves a married couple separating due to divorce. One spouse may be concerned about providing food and shelter, while the other may be anxious about how their friends or extended family may react. Each person perceives the crisis in his or her own way based on the life dimension that is affected. Assessing the life dimension affected by the crisis is therefore critical if crisis workers are to accurately target their interventions.

Crisis workers must also identify whether clients view the crisis as a transgression, threat, or loss. In each case, the intervention process differs. Take the divorcing couple, for example. If the spouse that has expressed concern about supporting him- or herself perceives a threat, the crisis worker would design an intervention that would help determine the reality of the anticipated problem. However, if the person perceives the situation as a loss, the crisis worker might help the spouse by identifying resources to locate lodging on a temporary, then permanent, basis.

POINTS TO REMEMBER

- Although often neglected, accurate assessment of clients' cognitive reactions is important because of the potential long-term effects if the crisis is not satisfactorily resolved.
- Crisis workers must distinguish their perceptions from clients' perceptions to accurately assess cognitive reactions. Failure to utilize clients' perception leads to minimizing clients' reactions, incorrectly assuming clients' reactions, and misapplication of similar cases.
- Cognitive reactions to crises are assessed as transgression, threat, and loss. *Transgression* refers to a demeaning offense against the client that is reported as currently taking place. *Threat* is viewed as a potential problem and reported as being in the future. *Loss* is something that has happened involving a perceived irrevocable loss, and is reported as being in the past.
- Cognitive reactions impact one or more of clients' four life dimensions: (a) physical—personal safety, food, shelter, and so on; (b) psychological— self-concept, emotional well-being, self-efficacy, and so on; (c) social relationships—family, friends, co-workers, and so on; and (d) moral/

spiritual—personal integrity, belief systems, values, religious beliefs, and so on.

- Crisis workers must be alert to clues that clients are suicidal and/or homicidal. Generally speaking, the more severe the reaction, the more potential there is for this type of behavior. If such ideations are suspected, crisis workers should act according to the standards set by their profession and community.

- Obstacles to the assessment of clients' cognitive reactions include the omission of information, inability to discuss anything but feelings or the actual crisis event, and clients' unfamiliarity with the interview process. Patience on the part of crisis workers is needed to overcome these obstacles.

- Most often, information needed to assess cognitive reactions is verbal. Nonverbal behavior such as eye movement can help corroborate clients' verbal reports, but should not be used exclusively to assess cognitive reactions.

- The closer in time to the crisis event, the more uncertain clients are regarding the life dimensions that have been affected by the situation.

- Clients' repetition of content with respect to a specific life dimension is a strong indicator that this is the area most affected by the crisis.

- Assessing the severity of cognitive reaction involves observing clients' ability to tell their story and their ability to recall commonly known information such as telephone numbers and home address.

- Severity ratings are assessed on a scale from 1 (No Impairment) to 10 (Severe Impairment). Ratings of 2 and 3 are categorized as Minimal Impairment, ratings of 4 and 5 are Low Impairment, ratings of 6 and 7 are Moderate Impairment, and ratings of 8 and 9 are categorized as Marked Impairment.

- When assessing severity, crisis workers should work from the Severe Impairment category (10) down the scale. When at least one of the descriptors is met, that generally indicates the category. If more than half of the descriptors are met, the higher rating of that category should be assigned.

STUDY QUESTIONS

1. What are some things you might do to differentiate your perception from clients' perception of a crisis?

2. What questions would you ask Mr. Everett to assess his cognitive reactions to the crisis of his daughter becoming pregnant? Would these differ from questions you would ask the wife whose husband died suddenly (described in this chapter)? If so, why and how?

3. What would alert you to use information given by others to assess clients' cognitive reactions?
4. What are some phrases clients might use that would help you identify whether they perceive the crisis as a transgression, threat, or loss?

REFERENCES

Aguilera, D. C. (1994). *Crisis intervention: Theory and methodology* (7th ed.). St. Louis, Mosby.

Akiskal, H. S., & Akiskal, K. (1994). Mental status examination: The art of the clinical interview. In M. Hersen & S. M. Turner (Eds.), *Diagnostic interviewing* (2nd ed., pp. 21–51). New York: Plenum.

Bednar, R. L., Bednar, S. C., Lambert, M. J., & Waite, D. R. (1991). *Psychotherapy with high-risk patients*. Pacific Grove, CA: Brooks/Cole.

Bloom, B. L. (1984). *Community mental health* (2nd ed.). Pacific Grove, CA: Brooks/Cole.

Bongar, B., Berman, A. L., Maris, R. W., Silverman, M. M., Harris, E. A., & Packman, W. L. (1998). *Risk management with suicidal patients*. New York: Guilford.

Browning, B. R. (1996). *An exploration of parameters of commitment in relation to stressors, stress response, and vulnerability to stress*. Unpublished doctoral dissertation, Northern Illinois University, DeKalb.

Callahan, J. (1998). Crisis theory and crisis intervention in emergencies. In P. M. Kleespies (Ed.), *Emergencies in mental health: Evaluation and management* (pp. 22–40). New York: Guilford.

Cormier, W. H., & Cormier, L. S. (1998). *Interviewing strategies for helpers: Fundamental skills and cognitive behavioral interventions* (4th ed.). Monterey, CA: Brooks/Cole.

Ellis, A. (1995). Rational emotive behavioral therapy. In R. J. Corsini & D. Wedding (Eds.), *Current psychotherapies* (5th ed., pp. 162–196). Itasca, IL: F. E. Peacock.

Ellis, A., & Harper, R. A. (1975). *A guide to rational living*. Beverly Hills, CA: Wilshire.

Emmons, R. A. (1986). Personal strivings: An approach to personality and subjective well-being. *Journal of Personality and Social Psychology, 51,* 1058–1068.

Folkman, S., Chesney, M., McKusick, L., Ironson, G., Johnson, D. S., & Coates, T. J. (1991). Translating coping theory into intervention. In J. Eckenrode (Ed.), *The social context of coping* (pp. 239–260). New York: Plenum.

Gall, T. L., & Evans, D. R. (1988). The dimensionality of cognitive appraisal and its relationship to physical and psychological well-being. *Journal of Psychology, 121,* 539–546.

Golan, N. (1978). *Treatment in crisis situations*. New York: Free Press.

Haan, N. (1993). The assessment of coping, defense, and stress. In L. Goldberger & S. Brenitz (Eds.), *Handbook of stress: Theoretical and clinical aspects* (2nd ed., pp. 258–273). New York: Free Press.

Herrera, R. (1996). Crisis intervention: An essential component of culturally competent clinical case management. In P. Manoleus (Ed.), *The cross-cultural practice of clinical case management in mental health* (pp. 99–118). New York: Haworth.

Hoff, L. A. (1995). *People in crisis: Understanding and helping* (4th ed.). San Francisco: Jossey-Bass.

James, R. K., & Gilliland, B. E. (2001). *Crisis intervention strategies* (4th ed.). Pacific Grove, CA: Brooks/Cole.

Janosik, E. H. (1984). *Crisis counseling: A contemporary approach*. Monterey, CA: Wadsworth Health Science Division.

Kemp, A. (1998). *Abuse in the family: An introduction*. Pacific Grove, CA: Brooks/Cole.

Kennedy, E. (1981). *Crisis counseling*. New York: Continuum.

Lazarus, R. S. (1993). Why we should think of stress as a subset of emotion. In L. Goldberger & S. Bresnitz (Eds.), *Handbook of stress: Theoretical and clinical aspects* (2nd ed., pp. 21–39). New York: Free Press.

Lazarus, R. S., & Folkman, S. (1984). *Stress, appraisal, and coping*. New York: Springer.

Maslow, A. H. (1970). *Motivation and personality*. New York: Harper & Row.

Meichenbaum, D., & Fitzpatrick, D. (1993). A constructivist narrative perspective on stress and coping: Stress inoculation applications. In L. Goldberger & S. Breznitz (Eds.), *Handbook of stress: Theoretical and clinical aspects* (2nd ed., pp. 706–723). New York: Free Press.

Morley, W. E., Messick, J. M., & Aguilera, D. C. (1967). Crisis paradigms of intervention. *Journal of Psychiatric Nursing, 5*, 531–544.

Myer, R. A., & Hanna, F. J. (1996). Working in hospital emergency departments: Guidelines for crisis intervention workers. In A. E. Roberts (Ed.), *Crisis management and brief treatment*, pp. 37–59. Chicago: Nelson-Hall Publishers.

Myer, R. A., Ottens, A. J., & Uden, L. (1994). Holistic assessment of rape victims. *Guidance and Counseling, 91*, 24–27.

Ofman, P. S., Mastria, M. A., & Steinberg, J. (1995). Mental health response to terrorism. *Journal of Mental Health Counseling, 17*, 312–320.

Okun, B. F. (1982). *Effective helping: Interviewing and counseling techniques* (2nd ed.). Pacific Grove, CA: Brooks/Cole.

Ormrod, J. E. (1999). *Human learning* (3rd ed.). Englewood Cliffs, NJ: Prentice-Hall.

Perlmutter, R. A., & Jones, J. E. (1985). Assessment of families in psychiatric emergencies. *American Journal of Orthopsychiatric Association, 55*, 130–139.

Pynoos, R. S., Sorenson, S. B., & Steinberg, A. M. (1993). Interpersonal violence and traumatic stress reactions. In L. Goldberger & S. Breznitz (Eds.), *Handbook of stress: Theoretical and clinical aspects* (2nd ed., pp. 573–590). New York: Free Press.

Rapoport, L. (1962). The state of crisis: Some theoretical considerations. *Social Service Review, 36*, 211–217.

Rapoport, L. (1965). The state of crisis: Some theoretical considerations. In H. Parad (Ed.), *Crisis intervention: Selected readings* (pp. 22–31). New York: Family Service Association of America.

Roberts, A. R. (1996). Epidemiology and definitions of acute crisis in American society. In A. R. Roberts (Ed.), *Crisis management and brief treatment: Theory, technique, and applications*. Chicago: Nelson-Hall.

Rosenfeld, M. S. (1984). Crisis intervention: The nuclear task approach. *The Journal of Occupational Therapy, 38*, 382–385.

Schunck, D. H. (1996). *Learning theories* (2nd ed.). Englewood Cliffs, NJ: Prentice-Hall.

Stanton, A. L., Tennen, H., Affleck, G., & Mendola, R. (1991). Cognitive appraisal and adjustment to infertility. *Women and Health, 17*, 1–15.

Sue, D. W., & Sue, D. (1999). *Counseling the culturally different: Theory and practice* (3rd ed.). New York: John Wiley and Sons, Inc.

Weaver, J. D. (1995). *Disasters: Mental health interventions*. Sarasota, FL: Professional Resource Press.

Yassen, J., & Harvey, M. R. (1998). Crisis assessment and interventions with victims of violence. In P. M. Kleepies (Ed.), *Emergencies in mental health practice: Evaluation and management* (pp. 117–144). New York: Guilford.

ASSESSMENT OF BEHAVIORAL REACTIONS

Maria is a married, 33-year-old Latin American woman with three children, two girls ages 5 and 8 and one boy age 11. She graduated from college, but has not worked outside the home since the birth of her first child. Maria called the domestic violence hotline Sunday afternoon and said she did not know where to go or what to do. She said her husband had been drinking over the weekend and had hit her a few times. The crisis worker immediately asked if Maria or anyone else in the house was in danger. Maria reported that she was not that afraid and that her husband never had hit the children, just her. She added that he did this occasionally, but only when he drank too much and that was only on payday, which occurred once a month. Maria quickly added that the violence took place only sometimes, not every time he was paid. In talking with Maria, the crisis worker discovered that she had been married for 13 years and had three children. Maria said her husband was 5 years older than she; they married after she graduated from college. The crisis worker learned that the violence had begun within the last year, but even from the beginning of the marriage Maria's husband exercised a great deal of control over her. He insisted she stay at home with the children and take care of the house. His reasoning, according to Maria, was that he earned enough as a lawyer to support the family. Maria had agreed to this arrangement and resigned her teaching position at a public high school, but since the youngest child was in kindergarten she now longed to start teaching again or return to school. She said the violence began shortly after she discussed the plan with her husband. Maria said she had thought of leaving her husband over the past few months, but simply could not work up the courage. She also said that over the past few months she had developed an interest in cooking and started experimenting with gourmet recipes. Maria said she wanted to assure her husband that she loved him. She added that she wanted her children to have a father and so would not consider leaving. Maria did express a concern that she did not want her son to follow her husband's example when he got married.

This case is not unusual for domestic violence. This problem can be found in families regardless of education, economic status, or ethnic background. The case does, however, present interesting issues for crisis workers assessing the client's behavioral reaction. How helpful would additional information be in assessing Maria's behavior? If additional information would be useful, what information would you want? For example, what if Maria's description of her husband's alcohol consumption is an exaggeration or overly conservative? What if Maria's desire to leave stemmed not from longing to simply enter the work force again, but rather to leave an increasingly cruel marriage? Given the description of the situation, is the client's decision to stay sound? Or, is Maria behaving in ways that are likely to be hurtful? These questions demonstrate that assessment of client's behavioral reactions is not straightforward. Crisis workers cannot assess clients' behavioral reactions without information regarding the nature of the crisis and intent of the behavior.

Assessing clients' behavioral reactions is critical for the development of interventions. By definition, clients in crisis are experiencing a sense of disequilibrium. Their usual coping mechanisms are not adequate to meet the challenge of the crisis. The resources commonly available to them also are not sufficient to resolve the crisis. As a result, clients engage in behaviors that are novel attempts to resolve the crisis. These behaviors range from doing absolutely nothing and being paralyzed to behaviors similar to a person who is fixated and obsessed, seemingly unable to stop. Some behaviors also may be dangerous attempts to resolve a crisis, such as suicide and/or homicide. At times, clients' efforts to resolve a crisis begin behaviors that take on a life of their own, wreaking havoc in clients' lives for years. Examples of this are alcoholism or entering into a relationship prior to satisfactorily resolving a crisis. Preventing these problems from emerging as a result of crises entails developing interventions that are based on competent, reliable assessment of clients' behavioral reaction.

This chapter outlines methods for crisis workers to use in assessing clients' behavioral reaction to crises. As in the previous two chapters, this chapter will begin with a discussion of crisis workers' role in assessing clients' behavioral reactions. In this section, the issue of understanding the meaning or intent of clients' behavior is addressed. The next section addresses the types of behaviors clients use while in crisis: immobility, avoidance, and approach. The final section discusses use of the Behavioral Severity Scale of the Triage Assessment Form (see Appendix B). As in previous chapters, this section will include practical suggestions crisis workers can use when making this assessment.

CRISIS WORKERS' ROLE

Assessment of clients' behavioral reaction is more than finding out what clients have been doing since the crisis. Simply knowing that a client has seemingly done nothing or has made several unsuccessful attempts to resolve the crisis is not enough. Crisis workers must see beyond the content of what clients report to truly understand clients' behavioral reaction. Accomplishing this task, that of listening to more than a report of behaviors clients have done, can be hindered by trying to gather all the details. Well-intentioned crisis workers can be misled if they agonize over every detail. Details are important, but focusing on individual facts will cause crisis workers to misinterpret the intent of clients' behaviors. Remembering to look at the overall intent of clients' struggles to resolve the crisis is essential in assessing their behavioral reaction.

Problems Associated with Accurate Assessment

Crisis workers often fall into the trap of making two premature assumptions when assessing clients' behavioral reactions. First, crisis workers assume they know what clients must do to resolve the crisis and do not listen to what clients have already tried. In other words, crisis workers make decisions about what is best without fully assessing clients' behavioral reaction. These decisions may be sound in selected circumstances, but crisis workers cannot simply prescribe a preset treatment without obtaining adequate information. Drawing from a list of prescriptive interventions to aid clients is not an effective method of helping. Clients are different, each with unique circumstances. What one client must do to resolve a particular crisis may be very different from what another client experiencing a similar crisis needs to do. Crisis workers can make suggestions and offer ideas, but clients are the ones who, in the end, are left to act upon those ideas. On selected occasions, crisis workers may need to intervene directly prior to fully assessing clients' behavioral reactions when the safety of clients or others is at stake. When clients are unable to ensure their own rights and/or safety, crisis workers can and must act. At these times, crisis workers function as caretakers to provide the support clients need to survive. However, in these circumstances crisis workers are encouraged not to foster undue dependence; as quickly as possible, they need to make efforts to facilitate clients' independence (Bloom, 1984).

The second trap involves crisis workers prematurely interpreting the intent or meaning of clients' behaviors. Too often, crisis workers judge the intent of clients' behaviors without adequately listening to the client's story. The case of Maria is an excellent example. In this situation, what is the intent of Maria's behavior? Is the purpose to preserve the family unit? Is the purpose to avoid taking responsibility for herself? Is the purpose to escape further violence if her husband discovers she has thought of leaving? Is the purpose to buy time in order to get a job or complete the additional schooling she desires? Any combination of these may form the intent of Maria's behavior. Yet, if a crisis worker merely assumes any of these possibilities, an ineffective intervention may be planned. A way to avoid making this error is to listen for what clients hope to accomplish by their behavior. The goal of the behavior provides a key to understanding the meaning of clients' actions when a crisis occurs.

Avoiding the trap of assuming the intent or meaning of clients' behaviors also involves recognition of cultural factors that may influence clients' reactions. Consider clients who are refugees from Southeast Asia, for example. If they fled their home due to political unrest, they might not seek assistance if they become a victim of a crime (Kim, Snyder, & Lai-Bitker, 1996). To crisis workers this reaction may seem unhealthy and unproductive, but for the refugees, given their experiences and culture, their response seems like the best course of action. Another example might involve clients who are gay. The meaning or intent of their reactions to a crisis might be different from that of mainstream, heterosexual clients. If, for example, a gay client is a victim of domestic violence, he may not contact a shelter or police for fear of being ridiculed. While this behavior may not be the best course of action, he has learned from past experience that other people do not understand his culture. African American reaction to a crisis also must be considered in view of their cultural heritage. These individuals may not seek assistance from authorities when in crisis due to mistrust. In the past they may have been mistreated and therefore will choose not to access those resources. What a specific reaction to a crisis means for this group might be very different from that of Euro-Americans client (Sue & Sue, 1999). Crisis workers must be sensitive to clients' culture in order to make an accurate assessment of behavioral reactions.

Ethical and Legal Concerns

Ethical and legal concerns are particularly relevant in the assessment of behavioral reaction because during the assessment process clients may disclose information about child or elder abuse, sexual abuse of minors, suicidal ideations, intent to harm someone else, or other equally disturbing material. Crisis workers can be caught off guard hearing this information; once it is disclosed, what are they to do? Are they legally required to report the information to law enforcement or other authorities? If so, do they stop clients, saying they must report what they have heard? Do they just keep listening and not inform clients they are required to report this information? Should crisis workers inform clients at the start of the assessment when confidentiality must be broken? If crisis workers do inform clients of these limitations, will clients hold back disquieting material?

The relevance of these ethical and legal issues for crisis workers is illustrated by the case of Maria. For a moment, assume Maria had indicated that her husband was hitting their children. What is the responsibility of the crisis worker? Because this situation would be considered child abuse, should the crisis worker report this information to the appropriate authorities? Should the crisis worker report Maria for child abuse on the basis that she has exposed her children to potential abuse? The law varies from state to state. In some states, only paid professionals are required by law to report suspected abuse, while in others volunteers must also report suspected abuse. In addition, states vary with respect to what should be reported. In some states only the slightest hint of abuse must be reported, while in others the evidence must be much stronger. The ethical issue of breaching confidentiality also is a factor in deciding when and when not to report. Crisis workers must ask themselves if the "hitting" of the children or Maria's inaction merits contacting authorities, thereby breaking confidentiality. Situations in which there is a clear, definitive case of abuse or non-abuse are easy to assess; the cases that are somewhere in between are the difficult ones. I recommend that before beginning as crisis workers, people make sure they know and understand the state regulations with respect to who and what should be reported. Crisis workers in training should also practice, through role play, handling situations where volatile information is disclosed. Finally, crisis workers should, prior to seeing clients, have a clear understanding of their agency's view of this issue (see Appendix A, which outlines legal and ethical issues).

Crisis workers' primary responsibility in the assessment of clients' behavioral reaction to a crisis is to ensure that no harm comes to clients or others. Crisis workers should be assertive and direct; the consequences of failure to assess the potential for harm can be extreme, including preventable suicide or injury to others. The role of crisis workers in this phase of the assessment is also to obtain information that will help point clients in a direction that will resolve the crisis.

BEHAVIORAL REACTIONS

The disruption of behavioral patterns is expected for people in crisis. The cause of this disruption stems from people's efforts, or lack thereof, to resolve the crisis. People work at putting their life back in order; they understand the practiced routine of their lives and appreciate knowing what to expect. At times, their efforts involve returning to the routine they established prior to the crisis. They want their lives restored, as much as possible, to the way they were prior to the crisis. Their attempts may involve pretending nothing happened or trying everything and anything to reestablish their lives. At other times, they struggle to establish new routines in response to changes resulting from the crisis. In these situations, the crisis has altered their lives to the extent that new routines and patterns are needed: A house is totally destroyed by fire; a divorce results in the need to find a new place of residence; the death of a spouse means new roles must be established within a family. These are just three examples of crises that necessitate the creation of new life patterns. Again, people may try to ignore the problem or may make ineffective attempts at putting their lives in order. The degree may vary, but people do react behaviorally to crises. Understanding and assessing this aspect of people's reaction, therefore, is an important facet in the development of intervention strategies.

Classifications Using Behavior

Research into people's behavioral reactions to crises can be traced to Lindemann's (1944, 1956) work with the survivors of the Coconut Grove nightclub fire. In his work with the survivors of this disaster, Lindemann discovered that reactions varied among individuals, but was able to identify two types of reactions—physical and behavioral. Some survivors of the fire later contracted medical diseases or disorders (e.g., ulcerative colitis and asthma), suggesting that they were not able to cope directly with the tragedy and instead internalized their reactions. In a sense, their behavioral reaction was that of avoidance or immobilization. That is, these survivors either actively avoided or ignored their loss, becoming ill in the process. Lindemann also observed behavioral reactions such as agitated depression, overactivity, hostility, and disturbances in day-to-day functioning. Some of these disturbances represent overt, maladaptive attempts to avoid the crisis; others represent a sense of immobilization. From this beginning in Lindemann's work, others developed their own systems to understand the behavioral reactions of people in crisis.

One system specifies a sequential series of behaviors people use to resolve a crisis (Caplan, 1964; see also Parad & Caplan, 1960). Caplan identified both passive and active behaviors people use to cope with crises. The first type, passive behavior, includes aimless activity, immobilization, and disturbance in bodily functions. The second type, active behavior, involves people trying unfamiliar problem-solving patterns to reduce the tension resulting from a crisis. These efforts meet with various levels of success, according to Caplan, but result in only a temporary lessening of the crisis. Others, such as Aguilera (1994), developed modified versions of Caplan's theory to understand people's reactions to crises. These authors assert that people engage in adaptive and maladaptive behaviors depending on which stage of the crisis they are experiencing.

Classifications Using Defense Mechanisms

Dixon (1979) used the defense mechanisms of psychoanalytic theory to understand people's behavioral reactions in crisis situations, describing these as

TABLE 5.1	COPING MECHANISMS	
Avoidance Behaviors	**Approach Behaviors**	**Immobilization Behaviors**
Repression	Intellectualization	Compensation
Denial	Rationalization	Restitution
Reaction formation	Identification	
Displacement	Introjection	
Projection	Sublimation	
Regression		

coping mechanisms to reduce tension, maintain a sense of equilibrium, and help people adapt when confronted with painful situations. These are classified into avoidance, approach, or immobilization behaviors (see Table 5.1). These become behavioral patterns people habitually use to cope with the world. When people become overwhelmed, however, these coping mechanisms are not effective because they may substitute for realistic problem solving. Subsequently, a sense of disequilibrium develops that is directly reflected in people's behavior. Crisis workers, therefore, must identify people's typical coping mechanisms in order to fully understand their behavioral reactions when in crisis.

Classifications Using Coping Mechanisms

The rubric of approach, avoidance, and immobilization can be identified in two other crisis models. As cited by Hobbs (1984), Bancroft (1979) builds on Lazarus' (1966) coping theory, identifying four principal types of behavioral reactions used to cope with crisis situations. First, problem-solving behavior is mature and adaptive—an active approach to resolving the crisis that involves the use of healthy behaviors. For example, when diagnosed with HIV, a person begins to read research reports regarding the treatment of the disease in order to secure the best possible treatment. Second, regression is an attempt to escape to the past to activate behaviors, especially dependent ones, that enabled the person to cope. For example, the person diagnosed with HIV might try to find a parental figure that would make the decisions about treatment and other issues arising from the crisis. Third, denial represents an attempt to avoid the problem by ignoring it or forgetting that it exists. Again, consider the person diagnosed with HIV. If denial is the behavioral reaction, the person would make no efforts to acknowledge the diagnosis and would function on a day-to-day basis as if nothing had happened. Fourth, inertia involves a response of immobility—an inability to function or identify any solution to the problem. The person with HIV might withdraw from day-to-day activities, simply waiting for the disease process to takes its course.

Koopman, Classen, and Spiegel (1996) found in their research with victims of disasters that people are (a) active problem focused, (b) passive problem focused, or (c) passive avoidant. Active-problem-focused people use strategies they think will resolve the crisis. For example, when laid off from a job, a person begins the search for a new position by looking in the newspaper, applying for positions, and using other methods that are calculated to secure a new job. Passive problem solving, on the other hand, is similar to immobilization. With this tactic, attempts to resolve the crisis lack potency and can be counterproductive. The laid-off person, for instance, might think about applying for a new job, but not follow through with actually making an application. People who cope with the crisis using passive-avoidant strategies pursue activities that help them avoid thinking about the crisis. The person who has lost a job, for example, might begin using alcohol or other drugs to avoid the problem.

Folkman and Lazarus (1988) identified two primary coping methods: (a) problem-focused coping and (b) emotion-focused coping. Problem-focused coping refers to attempts to resolve the crisis through actively changing the person–environment relationship. The person attempts to control the environment or change someone's view in such a way as to minimize the negative emotions caused by the stressful situation. Achieving this position involves a person actively approaching the crisis or stressful situation. For example, Maria, in the case at the beginning of the chapter, may develop a plan to seek protective shelter if she and her children are subjected to violence by her husband in the future. On the other hand, emotion-focused coping involves subjective changes in the person–environment relationship. The goal is to reduce the emotional tension resulting from the stress or the crisis. According to Lazarus (1993), two outcomes of this method are (a) a reduction of the stress through diverting behaviors and (b) a reduction of the stress through reframing the meaning of the event causing the stress through use of defense mechanisms similar to those described by Dixon (1979). These outcomes can be viewed as either adaptive or maladaptive, depending on the situation. For example, diverting behavior can be seen as adaptive if it involves activities that remove clients from the crisis temporarily and allow them to take a new perspective of the situation or to calm down. However, this same behavior may be maladaptive if leaving the situation causes further distress because the person cannot stop thinking about the problem.

Classification Using Ability to Function

A final approach to understanding people's behavioral reactions to crises involves assessing the disruption in their ability to carry out normal daily activities

(Hoff, 1995). This model assesses people's ability to function on a day-to-day basis as a sign of the intensity of reaction to a crisis. Such things as changes in social relationships, work habits, grooming, eating, and sleeping are considered as indicators of the disruption caused by a crisis. For example, a person may stop going to work or become unproductive while at work. Another person may lose interest in socially accepted grooming habits and start wearing the same clothes without laundering them. Others may begin acting on impulse, engaging in behaviors that are potentially destructive, such as abusing alcohol. Hansell (1976) identified other significant changes in day-to-day functioning, such as the avoidance of being alone, becoming clingy, or withdrawing from others altogether. While these behaviors are not directly related to attempts at resolving a crisis, they do emerge as a result of the crisis. According to this model, any change in social behaviors after a crisis should be assessed in order to understand people's reactions.

Common to these models of behavioral reactions to crisis are three types of behavioral reactions: (a) approach, (b) avoidance, and (c) immobility. Clients who react with approach behaviors to a crisis actively seek to resolve the problems caused by this situation. Their methods may be ineffective, but they are focused and intended to be helpful. Clients using avoidance behaviors actively seek to escape or dodge the problems associated with the crisis, attempting to move away from the crisis. A third group tries neither to resolve nor to escape the problems related to the crisis. This group of clients' reaction is immobility; that is, they are stuck. Clients behaving in this manner either do nothing or make self-canceling attempts to resolve the crisis. Self-canceling behaviors are those that cancel each other out. Clients will start to resolve the crisis only to abandon that effort too soon to see results, immediately initiating another effort to resolve the crisis. Research suggests that behavioral reactions in these three categories can be either beneficial in the resolution of the crisis and the development of effective coping mechanism, or detrimental, hindering successful resolution of the crisis.

ASSESSMENT OF BEHAVIORAL REACTIONS

Assessment of clients' behavioral reactions to a crisis is, on the surface, relatively forthright. For the most part, crisis workers will not find it difficult to determine if clients' reaction is approach, avoidance, or immobile. Generally speaking, common sense is the most effective strategy in understanding clients' reactions. By simply listening to clients tell their story, crisis workers can ordinarily discern the behavioral reaction to the crisis. However, common sense can mislead crisis workers if they fail to understand the intent of a behavior. For example, in the case described at the beginning of the chapter, the crisis worker could assess Maria's decision to stay with her husband as immobile, avoidance, or approach. If Maria is immobile, she is unable to make any movement due to the severity of the crisis; she is stuck, incapable of making a decision to do anything else. If Maria is avoidant, she is choosing to stay because she believes that no real problem exists. She might explain this by saying that her husband really does not have a problem—that he is just under stress, and when this goes away, so will the violent behavior. Finally, if Maria is approaching, she might believe that by staying with her husband, she can change his violent behaviors. Her attempts at changing her cooking style might be evidence of this effort.

Considerations for the Assessment Process

For crisis workers to appreciate the purpose of the behavior, they must understand the intention of the behavior, rather than only focusing on the outcome. This process is not as easy as it may seem, particularly if clients disclose disquieting information that clashes with crisis workers' values. The case of a client making a decision to discontinue treatment for cancer illustrates this problem. If the client decides to stop treatment because the side effects are too debilitating, the pain from the cancer is increasing, and/or treatment will only prolong the inevitable, how would a crisis worker assess the behavioral reaction? On the basis of the outcome? The consequence of suspending treatment is death. Should the crisis worker attempt to dissuade the client from making this choice because the crisis worker believes this act to be suicide? If the crisis worker makes an assessment based on the intention of behavior, would the behavior of the client be viewed differently? Appreciation of the behavior calls for crisis workers to refrain from imposing their values on clients and to consider both the intention and the outcome of the behavior in the assessment process.

Assessment of behavioral reaction involves evaluating clients' efforts, past or present, to resolve the crisis. Making an appointment to see a crisis worker or contacting a crisis hotline would not be included in the assessment, even though this behavior represents planful, creative efforts to resolve the crisis and suggests clients are motivated. Initially, setting aside these efforts can be confusing for crisis workers. However, crisis workers need to obtain as accurate a picture as possible of clients' efforts apart from support and assistance from people who are trained in crisis intervention.

As with the other domains of assessment, crisis workers should always be alert for suicidal and/or homicidal ideations. If any suspicion of suicidal and/or homicidal ideations surfaces, crisis workers must not be shy about asking if clients have thought of these acts as solutions to their problems. Inexperienced crisis workers might find it difficult to ask questions regarding this type of behavior. They might fear giving clients ideas or just not know how to ask this kind of question. Asking in a matter-of-fact tone during the course of the interview usually is effective. Clients are generally candid in their responses to these types of queries. If clients indicate that they have not considered these behaviors as

TABLE 5.2	TYPICAL CLIENT STATEMENTS	
Approach	**Avoidance**	**Immobility**
What if I did [this].	I thought about that, but I know it won't work.	I don't know where to start.
If I ever get my hands on him or her.	Don't say that, it will never happen.	I'm not sure what to do.
I'm tired of trying to get through this.	People tell me that I have to face it sometime.	I tried a bunch of things and nothing works.
I've tried that and it doesn't work.	I don't want to let go.	Nothing seems to work.
	I can't take it anymore.	People tell me to stop worrying.
		Why can't I get over this?

an option, crisis workers should move on. Yet, occasionally clients are not open about suicidal and/or homicidal ideations. Therefore, continued attentiveness is needed in order to completely dismiss this threat. Do not be afraid to ask about this issue again if clients seem to be having these thoughts. At times, it may take several inquiries before a client feels comfortable enough to disclose this information. If clients report having thought of harming themselves or others, crisis workers should attempt to determine the seriousness of this possibility. More is said on this topic in the section on assessing the severity of clients' behavioral reaction.

Usually the information needed to assess clients' behavioral reaction is communicated in the natural flow of the assessment process. No questions need to be asked because clients readily disclose their failed and inadequate attempts to resolve the crisis. They want to ensure that crisis workers recognize that support and help are needed. By enlisting crisis workers' assistance, clients safeguard themselves against the effects of the crisis. However, clients are not likely to use the words *approach, avoidance,* or *immobility.* Instead they will describe what has been happening and how they have reacted. Crisis workers must interpret clients' statements to assess the behavioral reaction. Table 5.2 contains examples of clients' statements and how these can be interpreted in terms of corresponding categories. Remember, however, that each client is unique, and, therefore, what may suggest a specific behavioral reaction for one client should not necessarily be interpreted the same for other clients. Crisis workers should be careful not to take isolated statements out of context, which often leads to inaccurate assessment. For example, it is not unusual for a client to make an isolated statement that could be interpreted as an attempt to resolve a crisis. If crisis workers focus on this particular statement, they may assess the behavioral reaction as approach. This client may make many more statements, however, suggesting that his or her reaction is avoidance. In this case, crisis workers would assess the client's reaction as avoidance rather than approach since the majority of the statements indicate that type of behavior. Again, crisis workers should listen for the overall tone of clients' reactions and not focus on solitary statements.

Types of Reactions

As noted, clients' behavioral reactions can be categorized as approach, avoidance, or immobility. The Triage Assessment Form: Crisis Intervention defines *approach* as behavioral reactions that are active efforts to resolve issues related to the crisis. Approach behavioral reactions may seem helpful, but crisis workers cannot assume that they are. Clinical judgment must be used to determine whether or not the behavioral reaction is helpful or detrimental. Assessing whether a behavior is beneficial (i.e., it promotes the resolution of a crisis) or detrimental (i.e., the behavior hinders resolution) involves making a judgment about the reasonably expected outcome of the behavior. If the outcome appears to be functional, to be socially acceptable, and to promote broadened coping mechanisms, the behavioral reaction is beneficial. For example, a family who is in crisis due to a natural disaster may react with beneficial behaviors by applying for emergency assistance provided by various volunteer and governmental organizations. Yet, the family is in crisis because these efforts fall short of the aid needed. Therefore, a crisis worker would assess the behavioral reaction as approach but offer help to the family to locate additional resources. There are times, however, when approach behaviors are detrimental to the resolution of the crisis. Take the problem of school violence, for example ("Experts Scrambling," 1998). Several of these incidents involved adolescents who were arguably experiencing some type of crisis. To resolve the crisis, these adolescents chose to open fire with various types of automatic weapons at what they believed to be the source of their crisis—other students. While this type of behavior is obviously not acceptable, these boys were attempting to resolve the crisis. In other words, they were approaching the crisis using behaviors that were detrimental to the effective resolution of the crisis.

Avoidance behaviors are defined as attempts by clients to flee from the problems associated with the crisis. These attempts may involve active or passive behaviors that clients use to defend themselves. Examples of active behaviors are placing blame on others, lying about the crisis, diverting attention away from the crisis, and hiding evidence of the crisis. Passive behaviors involve clients pretending nothing has happened and refusing to acknowledge any problems resulting from the crisis. As with the approach behavioral reaction, avoidance can be either helpful or detrimental to the resolution of the crisis. Determining the helpfulness or harmfulness of clients' behavioral reaction depends on two factors. First, as with approach behaviors, crisis workers must evaluate the potential outcome of the reaction. Will the behavior aid in or impede the resolution of the crisis? Second, timing is a particularly important factor for avoidance behaviors. For example, a woman's husband dies unexpectedly and she reacts using avoidance behaviors for several days. This situation is not unusual, and it is possible that given the shock of the crisis, she needs a few days to adjust to her husband's death. In this case, crisis workers would assess the woman's reaction as avoidance, but helpful. However, if after several weeks this woman is behaving as if her husband had not died, she is using avoidance in a detrimental way. Crisis workers must assess whether or not the behavior facilitates or hinders the resolution process.

Immobility is defined as either (a) the lack of attempts to approach or avoid problems associated with the crisis or (b) self-canceling behaviors that mitigate successful resolution of the crisis. Clients reacting in this manner often appear bewildered or confused by the crisis. In extreme cases clients may become catatonic. The more intense the crisis, the greater the chance that clients will react with immobility. They may not know what to do, so simply do nothing. Clients' coping mechanisms may have shut down or have proven totally inadequate due to the powerfulness of the crisis. To one degree or another, clients reacting in this way are vulnerable. They may be unable to or have limited ability to care for themselves. They are at the mercy of anyone who would choose to take advantage of the situation. Therefore, care must be taken to make an accurate assessment of this reaction in order to target interventions that will activate clients' defensive mechanisms.

Immobilized clients may also behave in a scattered and disorganized manner. Clients reacting in this way are similar to clients assessed as approaching the crisis in that they act—they do something. But, whereas approaching clients will engage in only one or two efforts to resolve the crisis, clients who are immobile will make many attempts to resolve the crisis, each of which negates the others. Clients reacting in this way may be flighty or erratic and impatient for results. For example, the family who is a victim of a natural disaster may become impatient when help does not come as quickly as expected. The family discontinues its efforts with that agency and moves to request help from another, then another, and so on. The net result is that the family receives no help because they did not work long enough with one organization. Again, this reaction can be either helpful or detrimental to the resolution of the crisis. As with avoidance behaviors, the potential outcome and timing are important factors in the assessment process.

A final note regarding suicidal ideations: Do not assume all suicidal thoughts should be assessed as avoidance. Circumstances do occur in which the most accurate assessment is that of approach. Crisis workers must understand the intent of the behavior in order to correctly assess clients' reaction. What is a client trying to accomplish by the behavior? Is the client trying to dodge responsibility or escape some type of painful event? If so, the behavioral reaction is avoidance. However, if a client is trying to cause others pain or hoping to provide money, through receipt of insurance, for others by committing suicide, the most accurate assessment would be approach. The importance of distinguishing suicidal clients' behavioral reactions in this way becomes apparent in the intervention process. For clients who are assessed as approach, crisis workers may help by diverting the energy needed to commit suicide into more helpful coping mechanisms. On the other hand, crisis workers may want to help clients assessed as avoidance find relief and support, or to reframe the crisis so that it is more manageable.

ASSESSMENT OF SEVERITY

Understanding the severity of clients' behavioral reaction to a crisis can be the most critical aspect of the assessment process because the reaction in this domain represents clients' attempts to resolve the crisis. These attempts, in some circumstances, may involve dangerous, destructive behaviors such as suicide and homicide. At other times, clients may use other behaviors, such as making decisions that change their lifestyle or abusing alcohol, that are maladaptive and will lead, if left unchecked, to additional problems. This behavior may represent an impulsive, "knee-jerk" reaction or possibly the lack of any overt reaction. In any case, this aspect of the assessment process is critical to ensuring clients' safety.

Characteristics of Coping

Crisis workers can use the characteristics of clients' behavioral reaction listed in Table 5.3 to assess the severity of the reaction. Are the client's attempts at coping with the crisis constructive? Does the client have suicidal and/or homicidal ideations? Does the client attend to personal grooming and engage in positive social interaction with family and friends? Does the client have normal eating and sleeping patterns? Crisis workers need to assess each of these characteristics, keeping in mind that clients are experiencing at least one of these characteristics to some degree; otherwise a crisis would not exist. Crisis workers should also be alert for interactions of these characteristics when the degree of the behavior is severe. For example, significant impairment in the capacity to maintain routine day-to-day activities might indicate suicidal ideations. Clients whose attempts to resolve the crisis are disorganized and maladaptive might also be having difficulty with tasks needed for normal daily functioning. Attentiveness to and recognition of these situations allow crisis workers to develop interventions that target relevant behaviors and help clients more quickly resolve the crisis.

TABLE
5.3

BEHAVIORAL SEVERITY SCALE CATEGORIES

Rating Value	Category	Descriptors	Characteristics
1	No Impairment	Coping behavior appropriate to crisis event. Client performs those tasks necessary for daily functioning.	Client's attempts at coping with crisis are constructive and not likely to contribute to additional problems. Client is unlikely to have suicidal and/or homicidal ideations, but, if present, these are only fleeting. Client attends to personal grooming and social interaction with others (e.g., family, friends, and co-workers) with little difficulty. Inconsequential disturbances in eating and sleeping patterns may or may not be present.
2 & 3	Minimal Impairment	Occasional utilization of ineffective coping behaviors. Client performs those tasks necessary for daily functioning, but does so with noticeable effort.	Client's attempts at coping with crisis are casual and/or passive. While these efforts are ineffective, they are not likely to contribute to additional problems. Client is unlikely to have suicidal and/or homicidal ideations, but, if present, these are only fleeting. Client forgets or overlooks personal grooming, and social interaction with others (e.g., family, friends, and co-workers) is difficult at times. Minor disturbances in eating and sleeping patterns may or may not be present.
4 & 5	Low Impairment	Occasional utilization of ineffective coping behaviors. Client neglects some tasks necessary for daily functioning, performs others with decreasing effectiveness.	If client attempts to cope with crisis, attempts are haphazard and possibly disorganized. While these efforts are ineffective, they are not likely to contribute to additional problems. Client may to make active attempts to resolve the crisis. Client may disclose suicidal and/or homicidal ideations, but neither a plan nor the means has been established. No time has been set to follow through with the suicide and/or homicide. Client neglects to perform personal grooming and withdraws from at least one social interaction group (e.g., family, friends, or co-workers). Disturbance in eating and sleeping patterns may or may not be present.

6 & 7	Moderate Impairment	Client displays coping behaviors that may be ineffective and maladaptive. Ability to perform tasks necessary for daily functioning is noticeably compromised.	Client's attempts, or lack thereof, at coping with crisis are impotent and may lead to more difficulties unless new, more constructive methods are begun. If client discloses suicidal and/or homicidal ideations, a plan may be partially determined but without the means; or, the means may be available, but not a plan. No time has been set to follow through with the suicide and/or homicide. Client seems helpless to perform personal grooming and withdraws from some social interactions (e.g., family, friends, and co-workers). Considerable changes in eating and sleeping patterns are present.
8 & 9	Marked Impairment	Client displays coping behaviors that are likely to exacerbate crisis situation. Ability to perform tasks necessary for daily functioning is markedly compromised.	Client is using ineffectual methods, either active or passive, to cope with the crisis that, if continued, will result in additional crisis or psychological problems. Client may also disclose suicidal and/or homicidal ideations with a definite plan and the means to follow through with those plans. However, the client states that these plans are to be carried out at a future time. Client unable to perform personal grooming and withdraws from all social inter- actions (e.g., family, friends, and co-workers). Decisive changes in eating and sleeping patterns are present.
10	Severe Impairment	Behavior is erratic, unpredictable. Client's behaviors are harmful to self and/or others.	Client engages in behaviors that cannot resolve the crisis. If suicidal and/or homicidal ideations are expressed, a definite time, along with the means, has been established. Client incapable of performing all tasks needed for daily functioning, including grooming, social interaction, eating, and sleeping.

Attempts at Coping   First, crisis workers need to assess clients' attempts to cope with the crisis; note that such attempts may be active or passive. In addition, note that calling a crisis hotline or making an appointment with a crisis worker is an attempt to resolve the crisis; assessment of this characteristic involves clients' prior efforts at resolving the crisis and so should not be considered in the assessment. Four basic questions address coping. First, has the client made any effort at resolving the crisis? The answer to this question may surprise inexperienced or novice crisis workers. Some clients simply do nothing, taking a Scarlett O'Hara approach to a crisis—"I'll think about that tomorrow." Most clients, however, do try to resolve the crisis. Assessment of this part of clients' behavioral reaction is generally clear-cut. Crisis workers only need to identify whether or not clients have tried in some way to resolve the crisis, being alert for subtle and seemingly indirect efforts as well as pronounced and direct efforts. Sometimes it may seem to the crisis worker that a client is making no attempt to resolve the crisis—but the client may believe that he or she *is* making such an attempt. A classic example is Maria, the client in the case presented at the beginning of the chapter. Maria began cooking gourmet meals just after the violence started. While this behavior is not necessarily directly connected with the crisis, it could be Maria's attempt to resolve the problem. She may believe that if she cooks better meals, her husband will acquiesce and allow her to return to work.

Second, are clients' behaviors constructive or destructive? This piece of information can help crisis workers assess the severity of the reaction because the more destructive a behavior is, the more severe the behavioral reaction. Again, the case of Maria is a good example. Maria's change to cooking gourmet meals is constructive even though it isn't likely to resolve the crisis. She is learning a new skill, possibly cooking more nutritious meals, and in general bettering herself. On the other hand, some clients' efforts are destructive. Maria might have chosen not to cook at all, which might have fueled the violence. Another example is a client who turns to looting or stealing after a natural disaster in order to replace damaged or lost possessions. Assessing the constructiveness or destructiveness of behavioral reactions calls for crisis workers to use common sense. The crux of the issue is determining the outcome of the behavior. If the behavior expands clients' knowledge, increases clients' self-concept, and/or is respectful of self and others, it is likely constructive. If, on the other hand, the behavior expresses intentional stubbornness, procrastination, or forgetfulness, does not respect the rights of others, and/or is immediately dangerous to self or others, it is likely destructive.

Third, do clients' behaviors represent adaptive efforts to resolve the crisis, or are they maladaptive? Determining whether a behavior is constructive or destructive is not enough; crisis workers must also judge whether or not the behavior is adaptive or maladaptive. While Maria's change in cooking style is constructive, it is not necessarily adaptive. To be adaptive the behavior must be a direct attempt at resolving the crisis. Since the cooking of gourmet meals is not a direct attempt at correcting the crisis of her wanting to return to work, it would be considered maladaptive. Maladaptive behavior, therefore, includes clients' efforts that are possibly passive-aggressive and/or do not directly address the problems encountered because of the crisis. You may be wondering if a behavioral reaction can be destructive and adaptive; the answer is "yes." Take for example the person who is looting after a natural disaster. The person is being destructive with this behavior; that is, this person is not respecting the rights of others and is committing a felony. However, this person is directly attempting to resolve the problems caused by the crisis, and therefore the behavior is adaptive. Generally, the more maladaptive the behavior, the more severe the reaction to the crisis. However, the same does not hold true for adaptive reactions. That is, just because the behavioral reaction is adaptive does not mean that it is less severe. The adaptiveness of a behavior is connected to the constructiveness or destructiveness of the behavior. Constructive, adaptive behavioral reactions indicate a less severe behavioral reaction to the crisis. The other three behavioral combinations (i.e., constructive-maladaptive, destructive-adaptive, and destructive-maladaptive) to a crisis indicate more severe reactions.

Fourth, how organized are clients' attempts to cope? Clients vary in their ability to organize efforts to resolve a crisis, depending on their previous experience with similar crises (Baldwin, 1979), precrisis level of functioning, personality characteristics (Blouin et al., 1985), availability of support system (Hobbs, 1984), the type of crisis (caused by nature or by humans; Cohen, 1990), and the degree of disruption to normal routine caused by the crisis (Bengelsdorf, Levy, Emerson, & Barlie, 1984). In general, the less organized the attempt, the more severe the behavioral reaction. Crisis workers must use clinical judgment in determining this. As clients tell their story, crisis workers should be attentive to the degree to which clients' efforts seem to be a sustained, focused attempt to resolve the problems related to the crisis. The more sustained and the more organized, the less severe the crisis. Do not confuse organization of efforts with success, though; efforts may be organized but maladaptive. Nonetheless, organized efforts indicate that clients are at least able to act; they are not totally immobilized.

The answers to these four questions form a gestalt that gives crisis workers information to assess the degree to which clients' attempts to resolve the crisis are constructive. As with each of the descriptors and their associated characteristics, crisis workers should exercise a great deal of caution before relying on any one answer to determine the severity of the reaction. Only when the answer is so significant as to present a danger to clients or others should it be used to determine the severity of the behavioral reaction. Consider, for example, a husband who happened to be in therapy at the time he discovered that his wife was having an affair with a coworker. He disclosed this information to the therapist, stating that he knew where this person parked and planned to be there one evening to put a stop to the affair by doing whatever was necessary. After a few questions the therapist learned that "whatever was necessary" meant the husband intended to rough up the other person. This behavior clearly represents a destructive reaction, and the therapist correctly assessed the severity of the reaction as at least moderate and possibly higher depending on additional information. Generally, however, crisis workers should not depend on responses from one question, but should utilize answers to all four questions when assessing the severity of clients' behavioral reactions.

Suicidal/Homicidal Ideations   The second characteristic concerns attempts to address the crisis that are harmful to either the client or others (Bengelsdorf et al., 1984, Kaplan et al., 1994). Assessment of suicidal or homicidal ideations is always part of determining the severity of clients' behavioral reactions. However, this does not mean crisis workers will invariably ask clients if they are suicidal or homicidal. Questions regarding suicidal and/or homicidal intentions need only be asked when crisis workers suspect clients have considered these options. If crisis workers are not sure or have any doubts, they should ask. The presence of these ideations directly impacts the assessment of the severity of clients' behavioral reactions. While many schemas have been developed to establish the lethality of these desires, intent (whether immediate or in the future), availability of means, lethality of means, and a definite plan are four variables always associated with the assessment of suicidal and/or homicidal ideations. In general, the more of these characteristics that are present in clients' thoughts, the more severe the behavioral reaction. Crisis workers must assess the immediacy of the intention; thoughts of doing harm to self or others that are more present oriented indicate greater severity. For example, consider a client who indicates the intention to commit suicide this afternoon while no one is at home. This situation is present oriented with a definite time set to carry out the plan and therefore should be assessed as Severe Impairment, or as extremely lethal. If, however, a client states an intention that suicide might be something to be considered later, with no specific timeline, assessment would be Low Impairment to Moderate Impairment, depending on other information. The availability and lethality of means should also be considered in evaluating the severity of the behavioral reaction. As you would guess, the more available and lethal the means, the more severe the behavioral reaction. To determine availability, ask how available the method of choice is. If the client has decided to commit suicide using a gun, does the client have one available? If the client has chosen to use drugs or jump out of a window, are the drugs available? Or does the client have access to a high enough window? Lethality of the means is also considered. A gun is always considered extremely lethal, while taking sleeping pills is not considered as lethal. Please remember, however, that all methods are potentially lethal and should be taken seriously. Finally, the presence of a definite plan as opposed to passing thoughts indicates greater severity. If the client indicates a specific time, place, and/or location, the assessment should be marked Severe Impairment. If the client does not indicate a specific time, place, and/or location, he or she should be assessed as Low or Moderate Impairment with respect to severity of the behavioral reaction, depending on other factors.

Daily Functioning   The third characteristic concerns clients' day-to-day functioning. The degree to which these routines are disrupted provides a valuable clue to the severity of the reaction (James & Gilliland, 2001; Rosenfeld, 1984). The more the disruption, the more severe the reaction. First, observe the client. Does the client seem to have bathed recently, or does the client have an odor? Is the client's breath fresh and hair combed? Does the client have circles under his or her eyes? How is the client dressed? A client coming to an appointment at a mental health clinic wearing a dirty, torn T-shirt, shorts, and no shoes suggests that the crisis has disrupted this person's typical routine.

Second, listen. How well do clients seem to be maintaining social and professional relationships? Social isolation and failure to perform work-related functions are both good indications of the severity of clients' behavioral reaction in this area.

Finally, crisis workers should attempt to gather information regarding changes in clients' eating and sleeping patterns. Any departure from usual habits is a manifestation of severity. Remember that some people eat more and others less when in crisis. Similarly, some people sleep more or less when in crisis. The key is a departure from typical day-to-day functioning.

Assigning Severity Rating

Like the Affective and Cognitive Severity Scales, the Behavioral Severity Scale contains six categories ranging from No Impairment to Severe Impairment. And, as in the other two scales, the anchor categories have one rating value while the middle four categories (i.e., Minimal Impairment, Low Impairment, Moderate Impairment, and Marked Impairment) have two rating values each. This system allows crisis workers to assess clients as either low or high in these categories depending on the number of descriptors they fit.

Crisis workers talking with clients using the telephone are at a disadvantage. They must make inferences regarding appearance and rely upon other information to assess the severity of the behavioral reaction. As the assessment process progresses, however, the distinction between telephone and personal contact disappears for crisis workers skilled in using the telephone. Experience and practice help crisis workers develop an inventory of questions that can be easily woven into the interview process. The use of direct, nonjudgmental questions is critical in establishing the rapport needed to conduct an assessment (Kleespies & Blackburn, 1998). Consider the case of Maria. While talking with Maria on the telephone, the crisis worker will want to determine if Maria's husband is abusing the children. To do this the crisis worker might simply ask, "Is your husband a child abuser?" Not wanting to label her husband, Maria might not be candid in her response to this question. The question, "Is your husband hurting the children?" would not be as likely to evoke a defensive response. Care must be taken to ask questions in a manner that clients will not find offensive or threatening. The crisis worker might ask questions regarding Maria's sleeping and eating habits, as well as questions about possible thoughts of hopelessness, to discern the severity of her reaction. Crisis workers can also use declarative statements as they listen to clients' stories. For example, the crisis worker talking with Maria, suspecting that there was a history of abuse at some level and that Maria had become accustomed to this behavior, could use statements like "My guess is you've become more and more isolated lately," or "I have a hunch that you are having trouble sleeping and eating."

Crisis workers should begin at the Severe Impairment category and work down when assessing clients' behavioral reaction, stopping when the client matches at least one of the descriptors in that category. Determining whether or not clients should be assessed at either the higher or lower value in a given category depends on the number of descriptors clients match. Clients matching more than one descriptor in a particular category should be assessed at the higher values. For example, Maria's behavioral reaction to her husband's abuse was consistent with both descriptors in the Low Impairment category. Maria was utilizing ineffective coping behaviors by not directly addressing the abuse issue, and she appeared to be having difficulty maintaining the tasks needed for ordinary day-to-day functioning.

Notice that distinctions between categories depend on the degree to which clients exhibit or do not exhibit behaviors needed to resolve the crisis as well as the degree to which they have the ability to perform tasks customarily needed to function in society. Clinical judgment is needed to distinguish between categories. Crisis workers need to look at the big picture rather than trying to account for every detail. For example, the crisis worker would probably not follow up if Maria had said that her son was on the football team because his team membership is not directly related to understanding the abuse. On the one hand, crisis workers need to be alert for subtle indications of severity; on the other hand, they need to be able to discriminate between meaningful detail and irrelevant minutiae, forming a larger picture of the situation as they observe and communicate with the client.

A final precaution: Clients assessed in either the Marked Impairment or Severe Impairment category of behavioral reaction are candidates for hospitalization regardless of their ratings on the Affective and Cognitive Severity Scales. Crisis workers should make every effort to ensure that these clients will not be alone until the severity of the reaction has decreased. In situations in which clients are having suicidal and/or homicidal ideations, crisis workers may contact the appropriate authorities and initiate the evaluation process for involuntary hospitalization. In less severe situations, crisis workers can encourage some type of hospitalization or enlist family and friends to stay with the client. Again, it is critical that clients assessed at this severity level not be left alone. Every effort should be made to ensure that these clients have someone with them at all times until the severity of the reaction abates.

SUMMARY

Assessment of clients' behavioral reaction involves a balancing act; crisis workers must strive to get the big picture while recognizing critical details. Trying to comprehend every aspect of clients' reaction is frustrating at best and, at worst, leads to ineffective interventions. Working with too many details fragments the intervention and can be just as overwhelming for clients as the crisis itself. Yet, failure to notice key details can also result in interventions that are not helpful. Interventions that fail to incorporate focal points of behavioral reactions can result in clients committing suicide, homicide, or engaging in other behaviors that may be unalterable. Special attention should therefore be given to this aspect of the assessment process. Determining which details are important and which are not can be difficult. Listening for information that seems out of context or impulsive can help in this process. Also, crisis workers should be attentive for behaviors that include an excessive emotional or value content.

In general, the key in assessing clients' behavioral reactions is identifying a pattern. Clients tend to resort to behavioral patterns as they attempt to resolve a crisis. They may repeat this behavior again and again as they work to remedy the problems associated with the crisis. Crisis workers have the task of perceiving this pattern as clients describe their situation. Accurate assessment depends on crisis workers' ability to judge the intent of the behavior. What is a client hoping to accomplish by engaging in that behavior? What does a client want to happen because of the behavior? These two questions are good ways to help crisis workers determine clients' behavioral reaction.

Because assessment of behavioral reaction is so important, crisis workers must carefully document clients' reaction. Documentation should include the assessment of the type and severity of clients' reactions, along with steps crisis workers take to ensure the safety of clients. In addition, crisis workers should record any consultation and/or supervision they receive in situations involving life-threatening behaviors because (a) such a record increases the likelihood that the assessment process did not miss critical information and that the intervention was appropriate, and (b) consultation and/or supervision in these situations helps protect crisis workers from malpractice through negligence.

POINTS TO REMEMBER

- The focus of assessing behavioral reactions is on the gestalt or overall intent rather than on details.
- Crisis workers should not assume they know what clients need to do to resolve a crisis or assume the intent of clients' behavior.
- Because sensitive information may be disclosed in the assessment process, crisis workers should be aware of their ethical and legal obligations with respect to confidentiality and reporting.
- A primary responsibility of crisis workers is to ensure that no harm comes to clients or others.
- Research suggests that behavioral reactions can be classified as (a) approach (attempts to resolve the crisis), (b) avoidance (attempts to ignore the crisis), and (c) immobility (doing nothing to resolve the crisis or doing things that are self-canceling). Depending on the crisis, each of these can be either beneficial or detrimental.
- The intent of the behavior rather than the outcome is crucial in assessing behavioral reactions.
- Past or present plans to resolve the crisis are used to assess behavioral reactions. Not included in the assessment is making an appointment with a crisis worker.
- Crisis workers should always be alert for potential suicidal/homicidal ideations and, if these are present, act according to professional and community standards.
- Assessment of behavioral reactions is typically through verbal disclosure by clients and is generally communicated in the natural flow of the interview.
- Assessment of the severity of behavioral reactions includes active and passive attempts to resolve the crisis, suicidal/homicidal ideations, the client's ability to maintain routine day-to-day functioning with respect to such things as personal hygiene and social relationships, and eating and sleeping patterns.
- Severity ratings are assessed on a scale from 1 (No Impairment) to 10 (Severe Impairment). Ratings of 2 and 3 correspond to Minimal Impairment, ratings of 4 and 5 to Low Impairment, 6 and 7 to Moderate Impairment, and 8 and 9 to Marked Impairment.
- When assessing severity, crisis workers should begin at the Severe Impairment category, or a rating of 10, moving down the scale until at least one of the descriptors fits. If more than half of the descriptors fit, the higher rating of that category should be assigned.

STUDY QUESTIONS

1. What behavioral reaction is Maria, the case at the beginning of the chapter, exhibiting? Why did you assess her in this way?
2. What are some situations in which the behavioral reaction of (a) approach, (b) avoidance, or (c) immobility is helpful or detrimental?
3. Describe key elements in determining the severity of clients' behavioral reaction.
4. How might clients' cultural background impact behavioral reactions? How would this influence your assessment?
5. Why is it particularly important to accurately assess suicidal clients' behavioral reaction? Are there other types of crises where this distinction is also important? If so, which ones and why?

REFERENCES

Aguilera, D. C. (1994). *Crisis intervention: Theory and methodology* (7th ed.). St. Louis: Mosby.

Baldwin, B. A. (1979). Crisis intervention: An overview of theory and practice. *The Counseling Psychologist, 8,* 43–52.

Bengelsdorf, H., Levy, L. E., Emerson, R. L., & Barlie, F. A. (1984). A crisis triage rating scale: Brief dispositional assessment of patients at risk for hospitalization. *The Journal of Nervous and Mental Disease, 172,* 424–430.

Bloom, B. L. (1984). *Community mental health* (2nd ed.). Monterey, CA: Brooks/Cole.

Blouin, J., Minoletti, A., Blouin, A., Nahon, D., Natarajah, M. A., & Croken, M. (1985). Effects of patient characteristics and therapeutic techniques on crisis intervention outcome. *Psychiatric Journal of the University of Ottawa, 10,* 153–157.

Caplan, G. (1964). *Principles of preventive psychiatry.* New York: Basic Books.

Cohen, R. E. (1990). Crisis counseling: Principles and services. In M. Lystad (Ed.), *Innovations in mental health services to disaster victims.* Rockville, MD: U.S. Department of Health and Human Services.

Dixon, S. L. (1979). *Working with people in crisis: Theory and practice.* St. Louis: Mosby.

Experts scrambling on school shootings. (1998, August). *APA Monitor,* pp. 1, 35–36.

Folkman, S., & Lazarus, R. S. (1988). Coping as a mediator of emotion. *Journal of Personality and Social Psychology, 54,* 466–475.

Hansell, N. (1976). *The person in distress.* New York: Human Science Press.

Hobbs, M. (1984). Crisis intervention in theory and practice: A selective review. *British Journal of Medical Psychology, 57,* 23–34.

Hoff, L. A. (1995). *People in crisis: Understanding and helping* (4th ed.). Redwood City, CA: Addison-Wesley.

James, R. K., & Gilliland, B. E. (2001). *Crisis intervention strategies* (4th ed.). Pacific Grove, CA: Brooks/Cole.

Kaplan, M. L., Asnis, G. M., Sanderson, W. C., Keswani, L., DeLaecuona, J. M., & Joseph, S. (1994). Suicide assessment: Clinical interview vs. self-report. *Journal of Clinical Psychology, 50,* 294–298.

Kim, Y. J., Snyder, B. O., & Lai-Bitker, A. Y. (1996). Culturally responsive psychiatric case management with Southeast Asians. In P. Manoleas (Ed.), *The cross-cultural practice of clinical case management in mental health* (pp. 145–168). New York: Haworth.

Kleespies, P. M., & Blackburn, E. J. (1998). The emergency telephone call. In P. M. Kleespies (Ed.), *Emergencies in mental health practice: Evaluation and management* (pp. 174–198). New York: Guilford.

Koopman, C., Classen, C., & Spiegel, D. (1996). Dissociative response in the immediate aftermath of the Oakland/Berkeley firestorm. *Journal of Traumatic Stress, 9,* 521–540.

Lazarus, R. S. (1993). Why we should think of stress as a subset of emotion. In L. Goldberger & S. Bresnitz (Eds.), *Handbook of stress: Theoretical and clinical aspects* (2nd ed., pp. 21–39). New York: Free Press.

Lindemann, E. (1944). Symptomatology and management of acute grief. *American Journal of Psychiatry, 101,* 141–148.

Lindemann, E. (1956). The meaning of crisis in individual and family living. *The Teachers College Record, 57,* 310–315.

Parad, H. J., & Caplan, G. (1960). A framework for studying families in crisis. *Social Work, 5*(3), 3–15.

Rosenfeld, M. (1984). Crisis intervention: The nuclear task approach. *The American Journal of Occupational Therapy, 38,* 382–385.

Sue, D. W., & Sue, D. (1999). *Counseling the culturally different: Theory and practice* (3rd ed.). New York: Wiley.

USING THE TRIAGE ASSESSMENT FORM: CRISIS INTERVENTION

To this point, assessment of the three domains (i.e., affective, cognitive, behavioral) has been discussed separately, as if crisis workers did one at a time. In practice, however, assessment in these three domains takes place concurrently. As clients bombard crisis workers with material that is sometimes relevant and sometimes not, crisis workers must sift through the information, gleaning the pertinent material in order to accurately assess clients' reactions to the crisis. If crisis workers incorrectly assess clients' reactions, intervention plans are not maximally effective, do not target the part of clients' lives most in need, and, in some instances, may be fatal if clients are suicidal or homicidal. Although assessment is ongoing throughout the intervention, in the first 10 to 15 minutes of contact crisis workers must make fundamental decisions with respect to intervention plans. What should be addressed first in the intervention process? How much support will a client need in the intervention? How direct should the intervention be? The elemental question, however, is, What can crisis workers do to sort through the information given by clients?

This chapter examines the assessment process in its totality; that is, assessment is discussed as it occurs in practice. The first segment describes the assessment process as it takes place in its totality, discussing the role of the counselor, identification of the crisis, assessment of the three domains (affective, cognitive, and behavioral), and how to use the severity scales. The second segment consists of three case examples based on real situations (but not actual clients).[1] Each case is unique, presenting crisis workers with a different slant on the assessment process. After each case study, the reasons behind assessment decisions are discussed.

CRISIS WORKERS' ROLE

Obviously, the role of the crisis worker is to make accurate assessments that lead to the resolution of the crisis. While easily said, this task is not as easily

109

accomplished. Crises are not simple, encapsulated incidents, easily understood and assessed. Rather, crises are complicated interactions of clients' affective, cognitive, and behavioral reactions as they attempt to resolve the crisis. These reactions are based in clients' patterns of coping, which have been developed through experience but have proven ineffective for the current circumstances. Assessment involves winnowing through clients' often chaotic account to obtain the information that will lead to effective interventions.

Initially, the crisis worker's role is to listen. Yes, just listen. Most of the time clients in crisis want someone to tell their story to, someone who will listen. Crisis workers can get in the way of clients telling their story in two ways. Giving advice without hearing the whole story is one way. Too often crisis workers jump in, offering suggestions that are meant to help but that can backfire because crisis workers have not listened fully to clients' stories. Remember that some clients have told their story to others, family members and friends. A safe assumption is that each person hearing the story has offered advice. Clients are probably tired of people offering advice; they want and need to tell their story. The result of falling into the trap of giving suggestions to resolve the crisis too soon is that clients will believe they have not been helped. Clients may say something to the effect that "I tried that, but it didn't work," or "Other people told me the same thing, but they don't understand." Both these statements are signals that crisis workers are not listening. Some clients, however, may not have told anyone about the crisis. Clients need to tell their story, which in and of itself is therapeutic. Patient, empathic listening will help these clients break their silence and feel safe to tell their story. For example, a teenage girl who is being sexually abused by a sibling or adult may not have told anyone about what is happening. Interrupting and giving advice too soon may cause the girl to leave prematurely or to not return for help. Another example is a man who is gay, but has not disclosed this to others. Giving suggestions about how to tell others of his sexual orientation before he has had a chance to tell his story may leave him believing he was not heard. In these cases, it is even more critical simply to listen. Failure to listen results in clients not getting the help they need.

A second way crisis workers do not listen is by asking for too many details, which interrupts the flow of the clients telling their story, results in them feeling frustrated, and generally means that the larger picture of clients' stories has been missed (Kell & Mueller, 1966). Admittedly, some details are crucial. For example, knowing whether clients who have suicidal ideations have made prior attempts or whether anyone in their family or a close friend has committed suicide is important. Other details are irrelevant. For example, information on past sexual experience would not be relevant in a sexual assault situation. Crisis workers need to make sure they are seeking information to more completely understand the immediate situation rather than to satisfy their own curiosity.

Yet, simply listening is not enough. Clients leave pertinent information out, gloss over other material, and say things that are confusing. Therefore, crisis workers' second major task is to ask questions that are focused on developing a better understanding of clients' reactions. Open-ended questions help clients explore their situation more fully, asking them to explain, describe, or clarify previous statements. These questions will most often begin with "what" or "how." However, at times these questions are posed in the form of clarifying statements, such as "Tell me more" or "Maybe you can say more about that." Some structure should be used in asking open-ended questions. It is important to remember that information regarding clients' affective, cognitive, and behavioral reactions needs to be gathered. Therefore, care should be exercised not to allow clients simply to drift away from giving the needed information. At times, crisis workers may need to interrupt clients in order to keep them on track. Remember that clients are in a state of disequilibrium and therefore may find it difficult to stay focused on answering questions. Strategies to bring clients back on task vary from gentle requests to direct appeals. Mild appeals should be made before using more forceful pleas.

Closed questions ask clients to give specific information. These questions generally are answered in one word such as "yes" or "no" or in short phrases. Closed questions are used more frequently in assessing clients in crisis than in general personal counseling situations. These questions ask for specific information regarding the crisis and help create a framework for crisis workers as they develop intervention plans. For example, in hotline calls involving domestic violence, crisis workers need to know if clients are in a safe location and if children are in danger. For crises involving medical emergencies, crisis workers may ask for specific information regarding diagnoses. Closed questions are particularly useful for clients who have reactions in the Marked Impairment and Severe Impairment categories. Not only does this type of question allow crisis workers to gather information needed to plan interventions, but the structure provided by closed questions helps these clients to gain a sense of control over the situation, functioning as an intervention in and of itself. Closed questions also allow crisis workers to gather information quickly in order to ensure clients' safety. Questions such as "Have you thought of committing suicide or harming yourself in some way?" or "Have you thought of harming someone else?" enable crisis workers to determine if clients are experiencing suicidal or homicidal thoughts. The most effective way to ask such questions is in a matter-of-fact tone. Clients are generally candid and provide honest answers when asked these questions. New and inexperienced crisis workers should rehearse asking these questions. The first time asking if a client is thinking of killing him- or herself can be disconcerting. Practicing helps crisis workers learn the best way for them to phrase the question.

Crisis workers must be able to deal with a lot of information quickly. The triage assessment model offers crisis workers a structure to help them collect and organize relevant information. In the following three sections, I discuss how to identify the crisis, how to assess the three domains (affective, cognitive, and behavioral), and how to use the severity scales. Keep in mind that these tasks are not discrete: Assessment of each takes place simultaneously. Crisis workers must be keenly observant as they listen to clients and have in mind what information they need to accurately assess clients' reactions. They must be fully present with clients. Things such as other thoughts, preconceptions, and past clients that might dilute crisis workers' concentration must be put aside.

IDENTIFYING THE CRISIS EVENT

The first section of the TAF concerns identifying the crisis event. First, the crisis worker simply records the event that was the catalyst for the crisis. What happened to cause a client to be in crisis? For example, in a case involving sexual assault, crisis workers may write, "Client reports having been raped by boyfriend following a party they attended." For a case involving a client who has been diagnosed with a medical problem, crisis workers might write, "Client reports meeting with his physician two days prior to this meeting and being told he is HIV positive." Be as specific and factual as possible, taking care not to interpret the event. Being exact is particularly important for crises that may give rise to legal actions (e.g., domestic violence, sexual assault, child abuse). Crisis workers must remember that clients' records may be needed in court as evidence for these situations and therefore they must accurately document clients' statements. However, in some situations clients cannot identify a single event as having given rise to the crisis. Instead, they describe a series of events that led to the crisis. In these situations, crisis workers should document each event and, if possible, report these in chronological order. Again, this step involves writing down the event(s) clients describe as having caused the crisis.

Having documented the event causing the crisis, crisis workers can move to the second step of this section—determining what clients view as the outcome of the crisis event. What do clients view as the problem resulting from the event? Crisis workers must take care not to make assumptions at this point. Instead, they should work to understand the crisis from the client's point of view. Errors are made when crisis workers impose their concerns on clients. For example, the client previously mentioned who was sexually assaulted may be more concerned with hiding this from her parents than with filing charges against her boyfriend. Assessment of the crisis as concern over filing charges against the boyfriend, as opposed to keeping the assault from her parents, would lead to different types of interventions. Crisis workers may sometimes need to suggest other issues that might be of concern. Doing this involves being attentive not only to what is said, but also to what is left out. Keep in mind, clients are in crisis and may not be able to think through situations. Clients may be focusing on a particular detail and need encouragement to explore other areas of their life that may have been impacted by the crisis. In these situations, crisis workers should draw on their training and experience to help clients gain a more complete grasp of the crisis. In the case involving sexual assault, for example, the young woman is focusing solely on keeping the information from her parents, but is missing the possibility that she may be pregnant or have been exposed to a sexually transmitted disease. Crisis workers can help clients like this think through such potential issues. For example, the crisis worker might ask the young woman about being pregnant, to which she might reply, "I haven't thought of that" or "I use birth control pills so that is not a problem."

Although there are two steps involved in the identification phase, they occur simultaneously. If clients do not volunteer information needed to identify and describe the crisis, crisis workers may need to ask questions, such as "What brought you here today?" or "What made you feel you needed help?" These questions will allow crisis workers to obtain the information needed to complete this section of the TAF.

IDENTIFYING DOMAINS

Crisis workers must also assess the three domains. Again, even though the TAF presents the domains in a linear fashion, crisis workers will be observing clients' reactions in all three domains at the same time. The TAF aids in organizing the often chaotic flow of information. Each page of the TAF deals with one of the three domains. Remember that clients will have reactions in each domain, so something will be recorded on each page. Do not be fooled into thinking that because a client's reaction in one domain is particularly acute, he or she is not experiencing reactions in the other domains. Clients have reactions in each domain, and reporting all three is essential to developing appropriate interventions. Failure to assess and report clients' reactions in each domain will result in incomplete and potentially harmful interventions. For example, neglecting to assess and report clients' cognitive reactions because the affective and/or behavioral reactions are particularly intense can lead to psychological problems in the future. Once the affective and/or behavioral reactions have abated, crisis workers may fail to address the cognitive domain unless this was assessed in the initial contact with clients. If not addressed, cognitive reactions may be reexperienced at a later date, appearing seemingly out of nowhere and due to a minor or unrelated incident. Again, remember that clients' reactions cross each of the three domains and should be reported on the TAF.

Notice that each section begins with directions instructing crisis workers to identify the particular dimension being observed. However, because crisis reactions are complex, with clients' reactions shifting, at times very quickly, crisis workers should identify every reaction that is observed and assessed. The instructions indicate that in these situations, crisis workers should report each, indicating which is primary, secondary, and tertiary, if applicable. Customarily, primary reactions are those reactions that are most prevalent. Be attentive to what clients report and want to discuss about how the crisis has affected and interrupted their daily lives. What feeling does the client talk about the most? How clients describe their initial attempts to cope and remedy the problems is also important. Listening for this information allows crisis workers to determine the primary reactions in each of the domains. What is talked about the most is the primary reaction. If clients do not disclose the information, or if it is not obvious, simple inquiries are usually effective. For example, a question such as "What did you do first to cope with the [crisis event]?" will elicit information regarding the behavioral reaction. To obtain information about clients' cognitive reactions, crisis workers might ask, "Since the crisis, have you been thinking more about your past, future, or just what is going on now?" Assessing clients' primary affective reaction can be accomplished by asking, "What feeling comes to mind most often when you think about the crisis?" Generally, however, the primary reactions in each domain are apparent by simply listening to clients.

Most often, the primary reaction is so strong that it masks other reactions in that domain. However, secondary and tertiary reactions, when and if observed, should also be assessed in order to complete the assessment process. Secondary reactions are those reactions that seem to intrude into clients' experience. That is, clients are aware of these reactions but see them as interfering with the primary reaction. For example, consider a client who has lost a spouse unexpectedly through death. The client's spouse may have left a lot of unanswered questions regarding financial matters. The primary cognitive reaction in the physical dimension might be that of "threat" since concerns regarding money may be paramount. However, the client periodically mentions the loss of the spouse's income. In this situation, the primary reaction is threat, while the secondary is loss. Crisis workers must be attentive to slight shifts in clients' focus during the assessment process, which may only consist of a few sentences or phrases made by clients. However, assessment of these is important in the intervention process, because as the primary reactions fade, secondary reactions may be exhibited. For example, the client who has lost a spouse to death may initially experience sadness/melancholy as the primary affective reaction. However, after a few weeks this client may begin feeling anxiety over financial matters or anger at the spouse for leaving business issues unresolved. Again, the primary reaction has a significant impact on developing an intervention for this client. Treatment would begin with supporting the client during the sadness, and once this feeling has begun to fade, treatment would address the secondary feeling.

Tertiary reactions seem to be on the fringes. Clients may be only remotely, if at all, aware of these reactions, which are typically masked by the primary and secondary reactions. If present, tertiary reactions become evident only as clients begin working through the crisis. As they begin to reestablish a sense of equilibrium, these reactions may come to light but are generally so limited that they do not cause problems for clients. If tertiary reactions seem to involve problems, treatment should address them. However, most often these reactions are effectively managed by clients because they have begun mobilizing their coping mechanisms at this point in the intervention.

USE OF SEVERITY SCALES

The information provided by the completed severity scales of the TAF indicates to crisis workers (a) where to begin the intervention process and (b) how direct an intervention is needed. The Domain Severity Scale Summary, which appears on the third page of the TAF, is reproduced in Figure 6.1. After crisis workers have assessed clients' reactions in each of the three domains, the values are transferred to the summary scale and then totaled. For example, if a client was assessed as a 5 on the Affective Severity Scale, a 7 on the Cognitive Severity Scale, and a 4 on the Behavioral Severity Scale, these values would be placed in the respective lines and totaled; in this case the total would be 16. These values are then used to develop appropriate intervention plans. The domain with the highest value—that is, the most severe reaction—is the area where crisis workers should begin the intervention. Crisis workers should intervene first in whatever domain is assessed as the most severe.

The severity scale summary also suggests how direct an intervention should be. Adding the scales results in values from 3 to 30; the higher the value, the more severe the overall reaction. Although the directness of an intervention exists on a continuum, basically there are three levels: (a) indirect, (b) collaborative, and (c) direct (James & Gilliland, 2001). The indirect approach, which corresponds to values between 3 and 12, can be termed the "you" approach. "What are you going to do to resolve the crisis?" Many times clients who assess in this range seek assistance just to confirm that they are proceeding appropriately. This intervention process most resembles personal counseling. The collaborative, or "we," approach is appropriate for clients whose values are between 13 and 22. Crisis workers team with clients to resolve the crisis. A technique useful for clients needing this level of directness is "priming the pump," named after the practice of needing to prime pumps to get water. In the past, when people got water from pumps they would, at times, have to save a small amount of water to pour down the pump. After pouring the water down the pump, they would begin pumping to form a suction and bring up more water. In crisis

Affective   _____
Cognitive   _____   FIGURE **6.1**
Behavioral   _____
Total   _____   Domain Severity Scale Summary

intervention, "priming the pump" involves offering clients a few suggestions about resolving the crisis. After hearing a few ideas from crisis workers, clients may be able to generate their own. In other words, they just needed a little priming to get started. The most severe reactions overall are the values 23 to 30. This severity level requires a direct intervention, or an "I" approach. Crisis workers may say to clients, "I want you to do this now." If clients are experiencing reactions at this level, they will usually readily accept the authority of crisis workers and comply with the request.

Please note that anytime clients are assessed in the Marked Impairment or Severe Impairment category (values of 8 and higher) on any of the severity scales, crisis workers should enlist the support of others to help the client. Even if only one severity scale is assessed at this level, crisis workers need to ensure that clients have someone who will stay with them overnight or longer if needed. If more than one severity scale is assessed this high, crisis workers should discuss admission to the hospital or a crisis stabilization unit for observation. If clients refuse, crisis workers should use clinical judgment to determine if other arrangements, such staying with family or close friends, will provide the needed attention and care to ensure the client's safety. Crisis workers should also consult with others on these cases and consider initiating involuntary commitment procedures if these are deemed necessary.

CONNECTION TO INTERVENTION

The TAF and the intervention process are directly connected. And, although this book is not intended to provide detailed information on interventions, some discussion is needed to demonstrate how this process works. Various strategies can be used as the basis for developing interventions in each domain. The degree to which these are implemented depends on the severity of the reaction; the more severe the crisis, the more intense or direct the strategy. Within each strategy, many techniques can be used; an exhaustive list of techniques is not given here, but examples for each strategy are provided that will help crisis workers get a sense of how these are used in the intervention process.

Affective Strategies

Strategies helpful for clients whose most severe reaction falls in the affective dimension should facilitate the understanding and expression of emotions, which in turn helps clients unravel feelings they may not be fully aware of. Crisis workers may need to provide direction in order for clients to become cognizant of their feelings as they work to resolve the crisis. The expression of emotions is also important in the resolution of crises. However, the expression should be appropriate and not create more difficulties for clients. For example, a client who has lost a job may be angry and in crisis. Expressing that anger is needed, but care must be used in how this is done. Exploding in an angry outburst at the employer may not be helpful. But channeling the anger to communicate indignation may be appropriate and helpful in the resolution of the crisis.

Crisis workers can use several methods to help clients explore and verbalize their feelings. Assisting clients to identify and take responsibility for feelings by using "I" comments can be helpful. For example, having clients start sentences by saying "I am feeling [angry, anxious, or sad]" allows them to begin understanding and expressing feelings. Crisis workers can also ask clients, especially children, to draw their feelings. This method is nonthreatening and often allows clients to begin to get in touch with those feelings they have discounted or ignored. Crisis workers must, of course, be sensitive to the cultural heritage of clients, recognizing that cultures differ in the valuation emotional expression.

Specific strategies are useful in each of the three domains. The first affective strategy is best termed *supportive.* Supportive strategies are used when clients need emotional help to resolve the crisis because they are plagued with doubts and uncertainty about their emotions. They may not be able to focus their emotions, or the severity of the reaction may cause them to become emotionally detached. Depending on the severity of the reaction, crisis workers can help support clients by validating their emotional reaction. Clients need to know that emotional reactions to crises are normal and that the need to express these is legitimate. The goal of crisis workers in being supportive is to empathize with clients; in turn, clients will sense the support and be more able to understand and express their feelings. Specifically, crisis workers can communicate to clients that having feelings is acceptable, and they can offer a shoulder to cry on. Crisis workers might also allow clients to become emotionally dependent for a limited time, until the shock of the crisis begins to decrease. Any technique that champions and strengthens clients' ability to resolve the emotional impact of crises is supportive.

The second affective strategy is *catharsis,* and involves techniques that enable clients to unleash their affective reactions. This strategy is particularly helpful for clients trying to ignore, restrain, and/or discount their affective reactions. Imprisoning these reactions internally results in inadequate resolution of the crisis and can negatively affect health. However, crisis workers must respect clients' cultural heritage; not all cultures value emotional expression. Some cultures are more reserved in the expression of feelings, and using interventions that compel people to express themselves may create another crisis.

The third affective strategy, *awareness,* is useful for clients who seem detached from or oblivious to their feelings. The affective reaction of such clients seems flattened or blunted. This is different from internalization. For example, a parent who has just experienced the death of a child functions as if nothing has happened. Another example is a client who is wandering around with a blank expression immediately after being involved in a near fatal accident or a natural disaster in which he or she was almost killed. At some point these clients will need to become aware of their affective reaction and have the opportunity to express it. Techniques include drawing, as well as showing clients pictures with people who are expressing feelings and having them describe what they see. Initially they may ignore the affective content of the picture, but after a while they begin to recognize the emotions being portrayed. Finally, clients are able to connect the emotions in the picture with their own experience. Care must be used with this strategy, however; clients may be in shock and need time before dealing with their affective reactions. Crisis workers should be sensitive to this need and be patient, allowing clients the time they need before using techniques that foster awareness of affective reactions.

Cognitive Strategies

Clients whose most severe reaction is cognitive benefit from strategies that help them to comprehend and organize their perceptions. Through the assessment process you may find that clients are unable to grasp the meaning of the crisis. They may be experiencing a sense of cognitive dissonance and be powerless to put the crisis into perspective. Clients may be experiencing difficulty in organizing their thoughts and be so overwhelmed that their ability to perceive the situation logically is impaired. In these situations, crisis workers can use the following strategies to help clients resolve their cognitive reactions. As with the strategies described for affective reactions, implementation depends on the severity of the reaction; the more severe the reaction, the more direct the strategy.

The first strategy involves *ordering* clients' thoughts. In this strategy, crisis workers use techniques that promote rational thinking. Clients in crisis can have difficulty ordering their thoughts and do not have a clear perception of the crisis. By promoting rational thinking, crisis workers can help clients set priorities rather than staying lost in a jumble of perceptions. Once organized, clients are better able to mobilize resources and coping mechanisms that have been unused or ineffective to that point. Problem-solving models can be an effective tool in helping clients order their thoughts. While this may seem elementary, remember that clients are experiencing a sense of disequilibrium and may not be able to use even the simplest problem-solving skills. Therefore, helping clients by going over a problem-solving model can be invaluable in helping them to order their perceptions.

A second strategy involves *clarifying*. While under normal circumstances clients generally have the ability to perceive the meaning of events, they may misread environmental cues when in crisis. In other words, their perceptions may be misleading, almost as if they had blinders on. Through clarification strategies, crisis workers can begin helping clients expand their capacities to discern events and start resolving the crisis. These techniques challenge clients to expand their interpretation of the crisis by offering new perspectives that encourage resolution. One way this can be used is to ask clients to explain what they have said. If, for example, a client says "Every time I feel warm I must have a fever and had better get some medicine," a crisis worker might ask him or her what "Every time I feel warm" means. It is important for crisis workers to pursue this as long as the client continues making rigid, uncompromising statements. The goal is to help clients see that other interpretations are possible and that locking themselves into one particular view may be paralyzing their ability to resolve the crisis.

A final strategy useful for helping clients cope with their cognitive reactions is to *delimit* their perceptions. Like clarifying perceptions, delimiting focuses on clients' perceptions, but instead of expanding perception, delimiting attempts to help clients regulate their perception. In other words, the goal of delimiting perception is to help clients stop catastrophizing. In situations such as this, clients might say something like "My life is over since I found out my spouse is having an affair," or "I got fired and now I'll never get another job." Crisis workers might counter by asking what the client means by saying "my life is over" or "never get another job." Have the client explain in detail what that means, thereby confronting the all-or-nothing perspective. This strategy helps clients to begin seeing that other interpretations are possible by forcing them to regulate their perceptions.

Behavioral Strategies

For clients whose most severe reaction is behavioral, crisis workers can use the strategies described below. These strategies are useful in helping clients whose behavioral reactions are endangering the safety of another person or themselves or whose reaction is making them vulnerable to exploitation. Again, the degree to which these strategies are utilized depends on the severity of the reaction; the more severe the reaction, the more direct the strategy. In the most extreme cases, involuntary hospitalization may be considered.

The first strategy is *guiding*, which involves helping clients locate and obtain the resources required to resolve the crisis situation. For example, crisis workers might give clients who have just been diagnosed with a chronic illness a list of support groups or a list of other people with that illness. If the behavioral reaction is severe, crisis workers might offer, if they are authorized, to transport the person to the support group. For frontline crisis workers such as police, guiding might involve helping crime victims locate organizations that provide restitution assistance, which minimizes monetary and property losses. I would encourage crisis workers to maintain a list of organizations that regularly provide assistance to people in need. This list must be readily available and up to date if it is to be useful.

A second behavioral strategy is *protecting*, which involves keeping clients safe from themselves and others. Whenever suicidal or homicidal ideations are expressed, crisis workers must take the necessary steps to protect the clients and others who may be involved. The degree to which protection strategies are employed depends on the lethality of the threats that have been made. The more lethal the threats, the more direct the action that should be taken. Also, when abuse of minors or the elderly is suspected, crisis workers must follow state reporting regulations. However, keep in mind that protecting strategies are not just for the extreme cases just mentioned. Sometimes, crisis workers can use protecting when clients are naive and unable to safeguard themselves against exploitation. Crises that fall into this category do not involve life-or-death situations. In these situations, crisis workers might offer information, encourage clients to seek additional opinions, or recommend that clients revise their plan of action.

The third strategy that can be used with clients whose behavioral reaction is the most severe is *mobilizing*. When using this strategy, crisis workers help to mobilize resources that will resolve and/or minimize the effect of the crisis. For example, when a person dies, a minister might mobilize the members of the congregation to provide meals for the family. In the case of illness, a minister functioning as a crisis worker might arrange for a person to get help around the house. Again, the directness of this strategy depends on the severity of the reaction. Again, the more severe the reaction, the more direct the intervention.

Intervention Model

The strategies described above fit nicely with the intervention model described by James and Gilliland (2001). Divided into two major parts, listening and acting, this model describes a fluid rather than mechanistic process by which crisis workers can help clients resolve crises. Listening involves three steps (but these are not discrete or linear). In the first step, defining the problem, crisis workers identify the crisis from the client's perspective. The affective strategies of offering support, encouraging catharsis, and fostering awareness, as well as the three cognitive strategies of ordering, clarification, and delimiting, can be used in this step depending on clients' reactions. These strategies help crisis workers assess clients' reactions to the crisis while also establishing rapport. In the second step, ensuring clients' safety, all the strategies described above are useful. Obviously, this step centers on safeguarding clients' physical as well as psychological safety. Particularly beneficial are the behavioral strategies of guiding and protecting, because they help clients access resources such as domestic violence shelters and rape crisis centers and by protecting them from harming themselves or others. The third step, according to James and Gilliland, is providing support. This step focuses on valuing clients and communicating to them that they are cared for by the crisis worker. All the affective strategies are helpful in this step, as well as the behavioral strategy of mobilizing. These strategies can be used to support clients' efforts as well as demonstrating to clients a sense of caring on the part of crisis workers.

The "acting" portion of the model also involves three steps. First, crisis workers help clients to examine alternatives, assisting them to generate options to help resolve their crisis. Depending on the severity of clients' reactions, all the strategies are effective in this step. However, the cognitive strategies can be particularly useful in helping clients sort through the myriad of possible solutions to resolve the crisis. For example, some clients may need to order their thoughts, while others may need clarification or delimiting of the potential solutions. Again, each strategy can be used in this step but must be tailored to clients' needs. In the fifth step in the model, making plans, clients organize what they need to resolve the crisis. Although all the strategies are useful in this step, the cognitive strategies of ordering and delimiting seem particularly constructive, along with the behavioral strategies of guiding and mobilizing. Techniques that fall into these areas can be used to help clients focus on resolving the crisis in a systematic manner. The final step, obtaining commitment, focuses on helping clients take ownership of the plan. The affective techniques of support and awareness, which foster clients' control and autonomy, are useful in this part of the intervention.

In summary, this brief discussion of strategies is meant as a primer to demonstrate the connection between the assessment process and crisis intervention. You are encouraged to expand and build on the suggestions that have been made. As you gain experience, your repertoire of techniques will also increase. Being an effective crisis worker means continually adjusting interventions based on the ongoing assessment process.

CASE STUDIES

The following cases were chosen to provide a range of possible crisis situations. Each case is a composite of actual situations involving clients in crisis. Different situations and types of crisis workers are utilized to demonstrate how the TAF can be used in a variety of situations. Each case starts with a brief introduction describing the client and setting. From there, client–crisis worker interactions and brief narratives are used to illustrate the assessment process. In addition, completed TAFs for each case show how crisis workers would document clients' reactions.

Case Study 1: Natural Disaster

The crisis worker in this case is a licensed psychologist who is trained as an American Red Cross mental health technician, currently providing services at a national disaster. The case involves a woman who was found by a person conducting a preliminary damage survey. She was taken to an American Red Cross center for help. Notice the patience used by the crisis worker throughout the interview. In addition, note how the questions asked by the crisis worker become increasingly specific as it becomes apparent that the woman's reactions were severe.

> Juanita, age 35, was found wandering the debris-strewn streets of her neighborhood by the American Red Cross damage assessment team within hours of the passage of a hurricane. When she was found, she was sifting through the rubble of a flattened home repeating the word *ebony* over and over. The worker who first saw her reported that she appeared dazed and confused. Tears streamed down her face as she tried to answer workers' questions about who she was and where she lived. At times, she appeared to be in a trance or dream state and was unable to verbalize her thoughts. The blood from a 3-inch-long laceration had coagulated on her leg, but she denied any pain. Juanita willingly complied with the Red Cross worker's request to leave the area with her. During transportation to the Red Cross center the worker who had found her reported that Juanita continued to repeat the word *ebony*. Upon reaching the staging area, a crisis worker was summoned to assess Juanita's needs and help her receive medical attention.

(Juanita = CL, crisis worker = CW)

While talking briefly with the Red Cross worker who was with Juanita, the crisis worker learned the basic information that the woman had been found wandering and repeating the word *ebony*. The crisis worker also learned that the woman had cooperated in agreeing to go with the Red Cross worker, but that she had not been able to provide much information.

> CW: Would you like to sit down?
> CL: *(CL sits without acknowledgment of the CW, crosses her arms over her chest and begins rocking herself.)*
> CW: My name is Craig. What's your name?
> CL: *(CL, eyes down cast, head bowed, begins sobbing, and after a short pause whispers in a barely audible voice.)* Juanita.
> CW: What's your last name, Juanita?
> CL: *(CL does not respond and furrows her brow.)*

Note that the client is unable to answer basic information about herself. The CW realizes that Juanita's cognitive reactions are in the Marked Impairment to Severe Impairment level. Additional questioning is needed to confirm this assessment. Although little information is available, the CW suspects that the severity of Juanita's reactions in the affective and behavioral domains are likely to be similarly elevated.

CW: Juanita, do you know what has happened to you?

CL: *(CL, still sobbing, begins wringing her hands, peers wide eyed off in the distance, and speaks haltingly.)* The wind was so loud . . . the roof was there and then it was gone. . . . I tried to hold her but I couldn't . . . she jumped out of my arms. . . . Oh the noise. . . . My house was just gone . . . *(CL jumps up and again begins repeating herself.)* Ebony . . . Ebony . . . Ebony . . .

CW: Who is Ebony, Juanita?

CL: *(CL does not respond.)*

CW: Can you tell me who Ebony is? Is she a friend, or your daughter?

CL: *(Still no verbal response. Client looks out the window and continues to cry.)*

The CW suspects that the CL's affective reactive is disrupting the CL's train of thought and decides to address this issue.

CW: Can you tell me what is going on right now with you?

CL: *(CL nods in agreement and begins sobbing even more profusely.)* I was so scared, I thought I was going to die.

CW: *(CW stands and reaches to comfort CL, but CL steps back abruptly.)* That must have been terrifying.

CL: I didn't know what to do. All I could think about was me. I just wanted to be safe and get out alive. I thought that I would lose everything. And I guess that I did, the only thing that was important, anyway.

The CW notes that Juanita is using the past tense; therefore the primary cognitive reaction is likely to be that of loss. The CW also knows at this time that three life dimensions involved are physical, due to the destruction of her home; psychological, due to her being unable to recall personal information; and social relationships, due to the loss of "ebony," although it is unclear at this time who or what "ebony" is. The CW suspects that the primary affective reaction is sadness/melancholy with a secondary reaction of anxiety/fear. The CL's behavioral reaction is still unclear.

CW: Can you tell me what happened?

CL: *(CL makes eye contact with CW, still sobbing.)* I couldn't move. I couldn't move. *(Louder the second time.)* I should have gone after her . . . Oh Ebony . . . *(CL sinks to her knees, reaching out to the CW as she does so.)*

CW: *(CW reaches out to CL and steadies her as they sit back down. CL grabs CW and continues to cry.)* You believe you should have gone after her? Who is Ebony?

CL: My cat . . . Ebony is my cat . . . she's only a kitten . . . I should have held her tighter . . . *(CL continues to sob).* I have to find her, let me go find her . . .

Because Juanita's behavior is disorganized, the CW assesses Juanita's behavioral reaction as approach but as maladaptive—it is not likely to help and may aggravate the crisis. The CW assesses severity at the Marked Impairment level, with a value of 9. The basis for this evaluation is that the CL is unable to care for herself and is engaging in activities that may exacerbate the crisis, but does not appear suicidal or homicidal at this time.

> CW: You believe you should have protected Ebony and you want to find her, but it is too dangerous to be looking right now. Once the area is safe, you will be able to return. Do you understand?
> CL: *(CL shakes head from side to side, responds in an irritated tone, but remains seated.)* I need to go, now!
> CW: Juanita, where do you live?
> CL: *(CL looks blank as her tears appear to be subsiding. After a pause she begins to speak.)* I don't remember . . . *(CL bursts into tears again.)* I'm cracking up . . . I can't think . . . I'm cracking up . . . I don't know what to do . . . I just need to find her . . . Ebony . . . Ebony . . .

The CW confirms that Juanita's cognitive reaction is also in the Severe Impairment range.

At this point the CW comforted Juanita again and asked her to come along to the first-aid station. Juanita complied without argument and also agreed to go to the hospital for observation once her wound was dressed.

Figure 6.2 summarizes the TAF completed by the CW. Note how the CW reported Juanita's reactions. Documentation was to the point, providing just enough information for another person to understand Juanita's condition. Specific information was reported to provide evidence for the CW's assessment. The rationale for assessing the severity of Juanita's affective reaction was her intense, continuous, open expression of affect without forethought. She also appeared to have difficulty controlling emotions and expressed the belief that she was going crazy. Because Juanita fit more than half the characteristics in the Marked Impairment range, a value of 9 was assigned. The primary affective reaction was assessed as sadness/melancholy due to Juanita's feelings about losing her kitten. A secondary affective reaction was recorded as anxiety/fear based on the CW's observation that during the interview, Juanita would lapse into discussing her fear during the storm.

The severity of Juanita's cognitive reaction was recorded as 10 due to her sole focus on the crisis event, her inability to recall personal information, and her obliviousness to personal safety. Her passive acceptance of directives from the crisis worker confirmed that this assessment was accurate. Because Juanita used the past tense to talk about what had happened, the primary cognitive reaction was assessed as loss. On the basis of the brief conversation, the CW judged that the life dimensions of physical, psychological, and social relation-

TAF

CRISIS EVENT:
The client was found sifting through the rubble of a destroyed house within 2 hours of the passage of a hurricane. She was looking for her kitten, who had jumped from her arms and run off in the middle of the storm as the roof of her house was blowing off. The client was dazed and sobbing when found. She was unable to identify her last name or her address.

AFFECTIVE DOMAIN

#1 SADNESS/MELANCHOLY—Client's affect was labile with periods of uncontrolled sobbing, especially related to the disappearance of her kitten.
#2 ANXIETY/FEAR—Client acknowledged being frightened during the storm and acted in a vigilant and hypersensitive manner during the interview.

<u>Affective Severity Scale Score:</u>   **9** (Marked Impairment)

COGNITIVE DOMAIN

PHYSICAL: **#1 LOSS**—Client acknowledged the destruction of her home.
PSYCHOLOGICAL: **#1 LOSS**—Client's sense of identity is disrupted. She can't remember her last name or address. Client perceived self as failure in caretaking her kitten.
SOCIAL RELATIONSHIPS: **#1 LOSS**—Client is extremely focused on the loss of her kitten, which is clearly an important relationship to her, beyond that of a material object.

<u>Cognitive Severity Scale Score:</u>   **10** (Severe Impairment)

BEHAVIORAL DOMAIN

#1 APPROACH (maladaptive)—Client is attempting to cope with the loss of her kitten by searching purposefully through the rubble and wishing to return to her neighborhood.

<u>Behavioral Severity Scale Score:</u>   **9** (Marked Impairment)

DOMAIN SEVERITY SCALE SUMMARY

Affective	9
Cognitive	10
Behavioral	9
Total	28

FIGURE 6.2

Case Study 1: Natural Disaster

---

ships were affected. Note that the assessment regarding social relationships was based on the loss of the kitten. Remember that not all social relationships are with people; at times pets and even treasured objects may be considered as part of this life dimension.

A value of 9 was assessed for the severity of the client's behavioral reaction. The rationale for this assessment was Juanita's efforts to find her kitten, which were likely to have exacerbated the crisis because of the extreme danger to self. However, this behavior was controlled and not erratic, and therefore not viewed as being in the Severe Impairment range. The primary behavioral reaction was assessed as approach, but as maladaptive. The basis for this assessment was that Juanita was actively attempting to solve the problem by looking for the lost kitten. Since this behavior placed her in danger, it was considered maladaptive.

This interview took just under 10 minutes. The questions asked by the CW were used to obtain as quickly as possible the information needed to assess Juanita's reactions to the crisis. Notice the patience used by the CW as he gathered the information, as well as how he avoided getting bogged down by details. By allowing the client to set the pace of the interview, the CW worker was able to obtain her trust and get the client the assistance she needed. As a side note, Ebony, Juanita's kitten, turned up alive and well 3 days later.

Case Study 2: Domestic Violence

Case 2 involves a domestic violence crisis situation. The crisis worker is a social worker who has been working at a domestic violence shelter for several years. She has established a good relationship with the local hospital and has been periodically asked to go to the emergency room to talk with someone the hospital staff believes is a victim of domestic violence. Before talking with the victim, the social worker was told by the hospital staff that this client had been seen several times for injuries during the preceding months. Each time the hospital staff suspected domestic violence, but the client was reluctant to admit this. Notice how the crisis worker does not panic when the victim mentions protecting herself with a gun. Instead, she works that into the interview later on two occasions in order to ensure the safety of everyone involved.

> Rhonda reported she had not slept for 4 days and 4 nights when she was treated at the hospital emergency room. She had arrived in an ambulance, which was called by the police during their response to her call to 911. This call followed an incident of brutality by her boyfriend. She was admitted for evaluation for the second time in 3 weeks, suffering repeated acute trauma to the abdominal area, where she had been kicked. Rhonda spoke rapidly to the ER nurse, launching a barrage of profanities describing her boyfriend, followed by a welling up of tears and short sobs, which rapidly dissipated into another verbal barrage. Rhonda's eyes were scanning the waiting room repeatedly when the volunteer from the domestic violence shelter arrived. The nurse seemed relieved to invite the volunteer and Rhonda to a corner of the room, where she closed the curtain around them as Rhonda sat down in a side chair and the volunteer perched on the examination table.

(Rhonda = CL, domestic violence shelter volunteer = CW)

CW: Rhonda, according to the nurse, a lot has happened to you in the last month. Can you tell me about it?

CL: *(CL flinches with pain as she sits up straight, clenches her fist, and begins to pound the arms of the chair, her eyes glaring.)* That son of a bitch Curt, that asshole, beat me up again! I told him I didn't have any more money to give him for drugs and he wouldn't believe me. That bastard grabbed my purse and when I wouldn't let go, he hit me. I should have left, but I was not going to give him any more money. Then he pushed me over the table and began kicking me, right in the same place he kicked me last time I had to go to the hospital. That prick!

The CW immediately begins to suspect that Rhonda's most severe reaction is affective. This belief is based on the intensity of the initial disclosure and the fact that it is affect laden. The CW chooses to pursue this direction in the following few exchanges.

CW: Sounds like this has happened before.
CL: Yea, right, like you didn't know. It happens all the time. Only this time he pushed me over the edge. I can't take this anymore.
CW: What aren't you going to take anymore?
CL: Him hitting me. I am tired of me trying to please him and knowing that no matter what, he's going to get pissed at me.
CW: You are fed up with him using and abusing you.
CL: You're damn right I am! I am getting a gun. I am not going to be treated like that again!

At this point, the CW decides not to pursue the issue of the gun in order not to jeopardize Rhonda's trust and rapport, although she will bring it up later. The CW knows that Rhonda cannot go anywhere until she is released from the ER. The CW believes the primary affective reaction is anger, but needs to confirm this as the interview progresses.

CW: Was this the first time you stood up to him?
CL: No, but every time I do it just makes him madder. We've been fighting since he moved in with me last Christmas. I keep saying I am going to leave, but I love him and I always take him back. When he is not using drugs, he is good to me and Shandon. Then he gets high and screws it all up. Eventually he gets straight and comes back and apologizes and I give in. I'm afraid to leave and afraid to stay. Pretty sick, huh?

Note the verb tenses Rhonda uses. She talks about the abuse in the present tense, indicating that transgression is likely the primary cognitive reaction. In addition, she mentions physical safety and relationship issues. Rhonda's affect also seems to be decreasing in severity as she talks about what is going on.

CW: You said something about getting a gun; is that the only way you have thought about taking care of yourself?
CL: (*Noticeably calmer, with tears in her eyes.*) No, not really, I've spent the night with my girlfriend a few times, and I've talked with my parents about moving back in with them, but that could be just as bad. When my

dad gets drunk he yells at my mom and my brothers and calls us names. I can't stand for Shandon to see him hit my mom just like I used to watch him. (*CL begins crying.*)

The CW notes that Rhonda has taken adaptive steps to take care of herself and her daughter, yet she seems caught by the anxiety of potentially losing her boyfriend, which also suggests some immobility.

CW: Sounds like you have been around violence often in your life, and it really upsets you. What goes through your mind most as you think about your situation?

CL: (*CL's sobs deepen.*) Sometimes I feel like I don't deserve any better. Then at other times, I want to scream how unfair it is. Men shouldn't do that to women. I don't want that to happen to my daughter. (*CL regains composure.*)

CW: Rhonda, before going on, I have to ask about the gun. You said you were going to protect yourself that way.

CL: (*CL shrugs her shoulders.*) No, that would only make things worse. Make me like him, and I don't want my daughter having to live with that.

Notice how the CW asks directly about Rhonda's mention of the gun. This inquiry is worked into the interview in a helpful way that promotes an increasing level of trust for the CL. Several exchanges take place in which Rhonda talks about her family and begins talking about her desire for her daughter to have a better relationship. During these exchanges the crisis worker confirms her belief that anger/hostility is the primary affect, but there is also some anxiety/fear, with occasional sadness/melancholy. During these exchanges Rhonda calms down, yet the CW assesses the severity of the affective reaction in the Moderate Impairment category with a value of 7. The reason for this assessment is primarily due to Rhonda's vacillation between intense affect and a more subdued affect.

CW: You want her to have better relationships than you have had. How old is she?

CL: Shandon is 4 years old.

CW: Where is Shandon now?

CL: She's with my sister, Corrie. I had a feeling he was going to explode tonight and I asked Corrie to take her. Corrie is an angel, she has been so good to Shandon. I should have listened to her about Curt. But I keep taking him back . . . why do I do that? It doesn't make any sense. I need to call my sister and ask her to come pick me up.

CW: I can help you arrange that after the doctor examines you. Where is Curt now?

CL: (*CL is much calmer, sitting back in her chair, rubbing her stomach, and grimacing.*) When the police drove up, he ran out the back door and jumped . . . or should I say fell over the back fence. The police didn't try to chase him but called in his description on the radio. I don't know where he is. Last time they found him at a bar. He was out on bail and back apologizing to me the next day.

CW: What do you need to be safe this evening? . . . I can offer you space at the shelter, which has an anonymous address and is monitored regularly by the police.

CL: *(CL sits up on the edge of the chair and clenches her fist again.)* What I need is to be safe, I just need to get the courage to walk away from the bastard and show him I'm not afraid!

These exchanges confirm the CW's assessment that Rhonda has been generally approaching the crisis in an adaptive manner. The severity level for the behavioral reaction is assessed at the Moderate Impairment level with a value of 6. The CW assesses the severity of Rhonda's cognitive reaction at the Minimal Impairment level on the basis of her ability to recognize the need to protect her daughter and her ability to think through not using violence to protect herself.

After about 20 more minutes, Rhonda was seen by the resident physician, who said that she had a deep bruise, but did not seem to have any internal organ damage. The resident prescribed a 5-day supply of a sleep medication and recommended that Rhonda check in with her family doctor the next day. Rhonda decided to ask her sister, Corrie, to let her stay over at Corrie's house while she took the sleep medication for the first time. Rhonda was smiling and occasionally laughing at the antics of an orderly flirting with the nurse when her sister arrived and the volunteer left. Rhonda agreed to call the shelter the next day and to attend a domestic violence support group the following evening. She also indicated she was not going to acquire a gun at this time.

Figure 6.3 summarizes a completed TAF for Rhonda. A unique aspect of this case is the low severity level of the cognitive reaction relative to the affective and behavioral reactions. Because the assessment was conducted soon after the latest incidence, the elevated severity level of the affective reaction suggests that Rhonda's immediate response is driven by emotions. Mitigating this response, however, is her overall problem-solving ability, reflected in the low severity level of the cognitive reaction. A complicating factor, however, is her threat to protect herself with a gun. In some cases, the moderate impairment for the behavioral reaction coupled with the severity of the affective reaction might suggest possible impulsive actions. The CW inquired about Rhonda's threat to get a gun several times during the interview and became convinced that she was not seriously considering this as an option, at least not at this time. Yet, notice that the CW documented this statement in the TAF. Careful documentation is critical in these situations in order to demonstrate that the appropriate standard of care was provided.

TAF

CRISIS EVENT:

The client was taken to the ER after being physically abused by her live-in boyfriend. She suffered bruises in the abdominal area. At the time of the interview the boyfriend was wanted by the police, but had not yet been apprehended.

AFFECTIVE DOMAIN

#1 ANGER/HOSTILITY—client repeatedly demonstrated angry emotions both verbally (cursing her boyfriend) and nonverbally (clenching fists, hitting the chair) and threatened to get a gun.

#2 ANXIETY/FEAR—Client acknowledged anticipation of danger and questioned the prudence of continuing to see her boyfriend even though she angrily denied fear of boyfriend. Client acted in a vigilant and hypersensitive manner prior to beginning the interview. Client has not slept for extended period of time.

#3 SADNESS/MELANCHOLY—Client cried over the history of violence in her family of origin and over the fact that her daughter is exposed to violence.

<u>**Affective Severity Scale Score:**</u>   **7** (Moderate Impairment)

COGNITIVE DOMAIN

PHYSICAL:	**#1 TRANSGRESSION**—Client believes the abuse is not fair.
	#2 LOSS—Client has suffered personal injury.
	#3 THREAT—Client realizes safety of self and daughter is at risk.
PSYCHOLOGICAL:	**#1 TRANSGRESSION**—Client is fed up with abuse and its unfairness to her.
	#2 LOSS—Client questions her mental health for continuing in the relationship.
	#3 THREAT—Client fears daughter will suffer as she did by observing family violence.
SOCIAL RELATIONSHIPS:	**#1 LOSS**—Client experiences a disruption of relationship with boyfriend and father.
	#2 THREAT—Client fears future loss of relationship with boyfriend as well as threat of violence.
	#3 TRANSGRESSION—Client believes she/women do not deserve violent relationships.

Cognitive Severity Scale Score: **3** (Minimal Impairment)

BEHAVIORAL DOMAIN

#1 APPROACH (adaptive)—Client is attempting to cope with the crisis by seeking medical care and a safe environment for self and daughter. She also threatens to retaliate in self-defense.

#2 IMMOBILE (maladaptive)—Client is often unwilling to actively remove self from the situation when emotions and risk of dangerous behaviors escalates and acts only after violence has occurred. She then returns to the relationship and does not make permanent steps to prevent further jeopardy, even though she recognizes a repeating cycle of violence.

Behavioral Severity Scale Score: **6** (Moderate Impairment)

DOMAIN SEVERITY SCALE SUMMARY

Affective	**7**
Cognitive	**3**
Behavioral	**6**
Total	**16**

FIGURE **6.3**

Case Study 2: Domestic Violence

The rationale for placing the severity value of the affective reaction at 7 includes Rhonda's extended period of intense negative emotions, which seem to be congruent with the situation, but which are controllable with effort. She also exhibited a sense of being overwhelmed at first, yet began to calm down after just a few minutes of talking with the CW. Some lability of affect was also observed as the intensity of Rhonda's affect escalated in relation to planning for the evening, but rather quickly subsided to a more stable level. Together, these reactions are consistent with more than half of those found in the Moderate Impairment category, and therefore a value of 7 was assessed. The angry outbursts led the CW to assess the primary affect as anger/hostility with a secondary affect of anxiety/fear. In addition, the CW observed a few instances of Rhonda expressing sadness, and therefore assessed a tertiary affect as sadness/melancholy.

The rationale for the CW's rating of the severity of Rhonda's cognitive reaction is based on several factors. First, she was fully able to recall personal information and easily followed directions. Although Rhonda's choice to remain in the relationship with her boyfriend seems questionable, she appeared to understand the nuances of her situation and was capable of recognizing and generally making competent decisions for herself and her daughter. During the interview, Rhonda was able to focus her thoughts as needed. She also demonstrated a sense of humor, suggesting that the cognitive reaction was not that severe. The CW, therefore, assessed the severity of her cognitive reaction in the Minimal Impairment range with a value of 3. On the basis of the interview, the CW assessed the crisis as impacting three life dimensions: physical, psychological, and social relationships. For the physical and psychological life dimensions, the CW assessed the primary reaction as transgression. This was based on the use of the present tense when Rhonda talked about these areas of her life. For the life dimension of social relationships, Rhonda talked about this area in the past tense, leading the CW to record that Rhonda felt a sense of loss. Secondary and tertiary reactions were also assessed in these areas, since during the interview Rhonda mentioned these occasionally. An assessment like this indicates that the client has spent some time thinking about the crisis and trying to resolve the problems associated with it.

The rationale for assessing severity in the behavioral domain as Moderate Impairment with a value of 6 involves the following factors. First, Rhonda continually places herself back in the relationship with minimal to nonexistent safety precautions. However, a second factor softens the impact; Rhonda takes the necessary steps to protect her daughter and acts to maintain her safety. Yet, overall Rhonda's attempts are likely to exacerbate the situation. A third but lesser factor is the disruption of Rhonda's sleep. While important, the sleep disruption is only one of many possible problems that could be experienced with respect to tasks needed to maintain her daily routine. Therefore, the CW did not consider the issue enough of a problem to warrant an assessment at a higher value. Assessing the primary behavioral reaction was complicated and dependent on the identification of the crisis. Since the crisis was identified as needing medical attention due to domestic violence, the CW assessed the primary reaction in this domain as approach and adaptive. However, given the history of the problem, a strong secondary reaction of immobile and maladaptive was noted.

Although the interview took approximately 45 minutes, only the first 15 minutes were described. During those first few minutes, the CW obtained the information needed to accurately assess Rhonda's reactions to the crisis. Again, notice how the CW did not over react when Rhonda mentioned the gun. Instead, the CW strategically probed this area a few minutes later in the interview. This pacing allowed the CW to strengthen the rapport with Rhonda and demonstrate a stronger sense of concern for her overall well-being. Although immediate and direct questioning of issues such as this is apropos in some situations with certain clients, a more patient approach is sometimes needed.

Case Study 3: Rejection

The final case involves a high school senior who was rejected by several universities to which he had applied. The latest rejection, which he received after a number of rejection letters over the course of a few weeks, put him in crisis. Since the young man was involved in his local church and trusted his youth minister implicitly, he went to him for help. The following excerpts are from the first few minutes of the initial interview with the youth minister.

> Fred, a senior, has been an outstanding student at his small rural high school. However, his college admission scores were only slightly above average. Fred applied to a number of prestigious universities in hopes of getting a scholarship to be a pre-med major. One by one over the course of 2 weeks, he received rejection letters from universities until he had only one outstanding application left. Fred was very involved with his church and sought out the youth minister, whom he had known for a long time, for consultation.

(Fred = CL, youth minister = CW)

> CW: Fred, you sounded very upset when you called yesterday. What's going on?
> CL: *(CL, staring at the floor, speaks softly in a monotone.)* I guess I won't be going to college. *(Tears well up in his eyes.)* I haven't gotten one single acceptance, and there is only one application left. I have been planning for college for the last three years and now it is all down the drain . . . *(CL's head lowers onto his chest.)*
> CW: That must really be disappointing.
> CL: To say the least. I really wanted to be the first in my family to get a college education. And now, I guess that won't happen. I tried so hard.
> CW: Sounds like you are really down.

CL: I can't seem to get my act together. No matter what I do, it turns out bad. It is almost like everyone has it out for me.

The CW observes the obvious signs of sadness/melancholy and makes a mental note to be alert for signs of suicidal ideations. The CW also decides to ask about behavioral reactions at this time.

CW: I can see you are feeling very discouraged, like you have no future. What have you been doing the past couple of days?

CL: *(CL makes no eye contact.)* I've been staying in my room mostly, listening to music. I even got high one night and I haven't smoked pot in six months. If my mom finds out she'll ground me forever. She keeps trying to cheer me up, she's even fixed my favorite meals . . . but I don't feel like eating . . . I just want to be alone and stay in my room.

CW: You said something about getting high. Tell me about that.

CL: You know, I just want to forget about everything. I thought that I had gotten over that, but now this. Getting high is the only way I can feel good about myself right now; the only way I can get away from everything.

CW: What are you trying to get away from?

CL: You know, not being accepted into college and disappointing my mother.

Fred provides valuable information regarding his behavioral reaction. The behaviors are active, maladaptive attempts at avoiding the problem. The CW also suspects the severity as being no higher than the moderate range, but possibly only in the Low Impairment category. Again, sadness seems to be the primary affective reaction.

CW: So you've been staying to yourself and you tried to make the pain go away with drugs. How did that work?

CL: *(CL looks directly at CW.)* I felt even worse when I got straight. Then I started thinking . . . I'll join the Marines if I don't get in college. *(CL becomes animated, sits up in chair and waves his arms.)* I'll join the Marines . . . they'll take me! My mom might be disappointed, but she'll get over it. After all, no one else in the family went to college.

CW: I get the feeling you know that getting high won't solve anything.

CL: I know that, but right now I just don't want to deal with anything. I worked so hard and for what, for someone to tell me I'm not good enough.

The CW is confident that Fred is avoiding the problem and is not using effective coping methods at this time. This, as well as the fact that Fred talks about his own failure, leads the CW to believe the affected life dimensions are psychological, involving the loss of his dream and vocational identity; transgression, involving the unfairness of the rejection; and threat, involving the ongoing attacks on his self-esteem. The CW is also hearing some anger in what is being said, but is unsure to whom this is directed.

CW: You seem to be giving up.

CL: Why not? I can't get what I want. Why not just join the Marines like everyone else in my family?

CW: The Marines probably would take you, and that may be a viable option down the road, but is that what you really want?

CL: I really wanted to be a computer engineer. It really sucks; I've tried hard in school and made good grades and gave up things I like to do this year to really apply myself. Damn it, it's not fair! I even prayed to be accepted, but where's God? He checked out on me, too. I don't know what I'm going to do with my life now.

This statements leads the CW to add the moral/spiritual life dimension to the assessment. Fred feels that God has abandoned him.

CW: You feel all alone in your dilemma, like even God doesn't care. Have you gotten any support from anyone?

CL: My friends don't know about it. My mom has tried to help me, but I tell her to go away and leave me alone. My dad hasn't said a word other than to yell at me for missing school yesterday. I think he is pissed off at me. He kept trying to tell me to set my sights lower . . . that I wasn't cut out to go to college. Now I bet he is laughing at me and saying "I told you so" and I will hear that from him from now on. I already feel low enough without him adding to it.

CW: That must be awful, thinking even your father is laughing at you.

CL: He's the kind that will say "I told you so." That will really get me. Then he and mom will get into a fight with her standing up for me and him telling her she's spoiling me. I just can't take it.

The CW adds social relationships as being affected. The primary reaction in this life dimension is threat; Fred is concerned that his father will reject him. The secondary reaction is loss; Fred feels that he has lost previously supportive relationships with his family. The CW also determines that the cognitive reaction is the most severe, since Fred focuses primarily on this domain.

CW: Sounds like his opinion is very important to you. What can I do today that would be most helpful to you?

CL: You've helped already, just by listening. Maybe you can help me come up with a plan on what to do next so I don't do something stupid . . .

The conversation continued for an hour, during which time the client denied he had any thoughts of harming himself or anyone else. He was able to express his feelings more deeply and to set up a plan to look at other less prestigious colleges with open admissions policies. The client also admitted that he was ashamed over smoking the pot and that he believed he was stronger than having to resort to drugs to cope. He agreed to make an appointment with his high school guidance counselor and to call the youth minister after he had done so.

Figure 6.4 summarizes the completed TAF for this crisis. Fred's situation illustrates how in a few minutes the CW can assess with accuracy the client's reaction to the crisis. By being alert to how the client responded to questions, the CW was able to identify the cognitive domain as Fred's most severe reaction. As the interview continued, this assessment was confirmed. In addition, the

TAF

CRISIS EVENT:
The client has been rejected admission by a number of universities.

AFFECTIVE DOMAIN

#1 SADNESS/MELANCHOLY—Client is tearful and doesn't make eye contact. Client speaks in a monotone. Client has been withdrawn and is not eating.
#2 ANGER/HOSTILITY—Client curses, threatens to join Marines. Client is cynical about his father and God.

<u>Affective Severity Scale Score:</u>   **5** (Low Impairment)

COGNITIVE DOMAIN

PSYCHOLOGICAL:	**#1 LOSS**—Client suffers the loss of his long-term dream and vocational identity **#2 TRANSGRESSION**—Client believes his rejection is not fair. **#3 THREAT**—Client anticipates ongoing attacks on self-esteem based on father's opinion.
SOCIAL RELATIONSHIPS:	**#1 THREAT**—Client anticipates ongoing disruptions in father's acceptance of him. Client believes he is currently being ridiculed by father. **#2 LOSS**—Client experiences father's distance from him and his own withdrawal from the support of family and friends.
MORAL/SPIRITUAL:	**#1 LOSS**—Client feels abandoned by God.

<u>Cognitive Severity Scale Score:</u>   **5** (Low Impairment)

BEHAVIORAL DOMAIN

#1 AVOIDANCE—Client is isolating self from emotional support and facilitative consultation that could allow him to reframe his dilemma. Client is attempting to cope by using drugs and repressing emotions.
#1 APPROACH—Client sought out the counsel of the youth minister to begin to address his situation.

<u>Behavioral Severity Scale Score:</u>   **4** (Low Impairment)

DOMAIN SEVERITY SCALE SUMMARY

Affective	4
Cognitive	5
Behavioral	<u>4</u>
Total	<u>**13**</u>

FIGURE **6.4**

Case Study 3: Rejection

CW was able to glean enough information in this short exchange to assess Fred's affective and behavioral reactions.

Fred's primary affective reaction was assessed as sadness/melancholy, with a secondary reaction as anger/hostility. The assessment of the primary affect was based on Fred's demeanor and his expression of sadness during the first few interchanges of the interview. The anger become apparent when Fred discussed his desire to join the Marines, which was viewed as a passive-aggressive attempt to cope with the situation. The rationale for assessing the severity of the affective reaction in the Low Impairment category with the value of 4 involves two things. First, Fred's sadness seems appropriate given the situation. He was facing losing a dream and, therefore, some sadness can be expected. Fred also could express his emotions without loss of control, and the CW observed no lability of affect. These characteristics placed the reaction at the low end of Low Impairment.

The life dimensions affected by this crisis were psychological, social relationships, and moral/spiritual. For the dimensions of psychological and moral/ spiritual, the primary reaction was loss. Fred discussed these in the past tense, suggesting he was perceiving a loss. Secondary and tertiary reactions were also identified in the psychological life dimension. Fred mentioned these, but they appeared only as tangential. With respect to social relationships, Fred perceived a potential for harm; thus the primary reaction was threat. The severity of these reactions was assessed at 5 in the Low Impairment category. The rationale for this assessment is based on Fred's ability to recall personal information and follow directions. He understood the need to care better for himself, but postponed efforts to eat and seek social support. Fred's perception of the finality of his loss appears reactive and obsessive and may differ from the reality that he can ultimately be accepted to college. However, his reaction was not significantly different from what is to be expected for an adolescent.

The severity of Fred's behavioral reaction was assessed as 4 in the Low Impairment category. The basis for this assessment involves Fred's use of a haphazard approach to coping. His disclosure of using drugs was of concern but did not appear to be frequent enough to warrant additional assessment. Fred's thoughts of joining the Marines also will not likely to contribute to additional problems and therefore was not assessed as such. His isolation and not eating did not seem clinically significant, but if continued, this would become increasingly important, as would continued reliance on drugs. Fred was not seeking ways to directly address his crisis; therefore the primary reaction was avoidance, which in this case would be considered maladaptive. No other reaction was observed by the CW.

This case is an example of how in the first few minutes of an interview, clients provide an adequate amount of information for assessment. Crisis workers must be alert to hear this information and make accurate assessments. This situation also illustrates the need for crisis workers not to become sidetracked or to allow their values to interfere with the interview process. When Fred disclosed his feelings of abandonment by God, the crisis worker, in this case the youth minister, could have easily focused on that issue and entered into a theological debate with Fred. Instead, the crisis worker correctly focused on Fred's affective reaction and asked if he had found support elsewhere. This permitted the crisis worker to obtain information regarding the need to activate support if Fred were to become suicidal.

Summary

Assessment for crisis intervention is an ongoing process that continually monitors clients' reactions. Unlike other assessment methods (i.e., diagnostic, standardized testing, psychosocial histories), crisis assessment must translate immediately and directly into interventions. Crisis workers must make accurate assessments if interventions are to be timely and efficient. Crisis workers must actively direct the assessment process if the information needed to plan interventions is to be obtained. However, actively directing the assessment does not mean pushing clients beyond their capacity at that moment. Critical to the process is an intuitive sense of pacing that cultivates trust and rapport with clients. In addition, crisis workers must have a model by which they can gather the information required to help clients. The TAF offers such a model; it is holistic in that it covers the affective, cognitive, and behavioral domains, as well as providing a means of assessing severity in these areas.

The three cases presented here are representative of clients who are in crisis. In each case, the TAF was used to understand and assess clients' reactions. The crisis workers worked swiftly and skillfully to grasp the client's reactions. Quick thinking and active listening allowed the crisis workers to assess accurately the clients' reactions and thereby develop appropriate intervention strategies. In crisis intervention, minutes and even seconds count. Therefore, crisis workers must be adept at quickly identifying information that will facilitate the assessment process. Care must be used to avoid becoming ensnared in irrelevant details. This book provides a basic primer for crisis workers, but of course practice, training, experience, and consultation are necessary to develop the skills needed to help clients in crisis. Unfortunately, most academic programs neglect, through either choice or oversight, training students in this area. Most training is acquired through on-the-job training or through workshops. Volunteers are frequently better trained than professionals in crisis intervention. I encourage you to use this book as a springboard to further your skills in crisis assessment and intervention.

Points to Remember

- Giving advice and asking for too many details can get in the way of listening to clients tell their story.
- Asking open and closed questions helps to clarify clients' stories.
- The first step in the assessment process is to identify the crisis event by determining the catalyst for the crisis and to specify what clients view as the crisis.
- The second step in crisis assessment is to identify clients' affective, cognitive, and behavioral reactions to the crisis. Remember, clients have reactions in each area regardless of the severity in any one area.
- The third step in assessing clients' reactions is to rate the severity of these reactions. Severity of reactions indicates two things: (a) where to begin the intervention process and (b) how direct the intervention should be.
- Crisis workers should begin the intervention process in the domain with the most severe reaction.
- The sum of the severity ratings reveals how direct the intervention should be, with the more severe reactions requiring a more direct approach. As a guideline, sums from 3 to 12 indicate an indirect approach—What can "you" do about the crisis? Sums from 13 to 22 indicate a collaborative approach—How can "we" work together to resolve the crisis? Sums 23 and above indicate a direct approach—"I" would like you to do this right now to help resolve the crisis.
- Note that whenever clients are assessed in the Marked Impairment and Severe Impairment" categories (i.e., ratings of 8 or above), crisis workers should seek consultation. If more that one severity scale is in this range, hospitalization should be considered and discussed with the client.
- Affective strategies in crisis intervention are (a) supportive strategies, (b) catharsis, and (c) awareness.
- Cognitive strategies in crisis intervention are (a) ordering, (b) clarifying, and (c) delimiting.
- Behavioral strategies in crisis intervention are (a) guiding, (b) protecting, and (c) mobilizing.

Study Questions

1. What are some skills that are useful for assessing clients in crisis?
2. What are some questions that can be asked to obtain the information needed to assess clients who are in crisis?
3. Describe how the Domain Severity Scale Summary can be used. How can this be the springboard to the planning of effective interventions?

4. What are some interventions that you might develop for the three cases presented in this chapter?

REFERENCES

James, R. K., & Gilliland, B. E. (2001). *Crisis intervention strategies* (4th ed.). Monterey, CA: Brooks/Cole.

Kell, B. L., & Mueller, W. J. (1966). *Impact and change: A study of counseling relationships.* Englewood Cliffs, NJ: Prentice-Hall.

NOTE

1. I want to express my thanks to R. Craig Williams, Ph.D, for helping to coauthor the three cases used in this chapter. His experience and assistance were invaluable in completing this portion of the chapter. Dr. Williams also helped to develop the Triage Assessment Form: Crisis Intervention and is currently in private practice in the Wilmington, Delaware area.

Ethical and Legal Issues A

Daily, ethical questions arise concerning specific situations for crisis workers: Should confidentiality be maintained if a client reports a crime to a volunteer crisis worker? What is the ethical responsibility of a volunteer crisis worker if a client expresses a desire to become intimate with him or her? Can a volunteer crisis worker claim privileged communication if subpoenaed to testify in court? What is the responsibility of volunteer crisis workers with respect to using their values as benchmarks when talking with clients? A few years ago, the news program *Prime Time Live* told the story of a woman who was seduced by a supposedly reputable counselor into an intimate relationship. This woman contacted the counselor after leaving a shelter for abused women. Exposed and vulnerable, she had only one session with the counselor prior to becoming sexually intimate. The outcome of the story was that the counselor was prosecuted under a law that prohibited this type of relationship with clients. However, since the person was not a member of a professional organization such as the American Psychological Association, the National Association of Social Workers, or the American Counseling Association, no ethical standards were directly applicable.

Anyone working with the public must be careful to ensure that ethical standards and legal statutes are followed. This is especially true when one is helping people in crisis, who are experiencing a sense of disequilibrium and may be vulnerable to suggestions. Unscrupulous people can and do prey on this group, often taking advantage of them for personal profit. Yet, except for suicidal or homicidal clients and situations involving abuse, little attention is generally given to the ethical and legal issues involved in helping someone in crisis. Professional human service workers such as licensed psychologists, social workers, counselors, nurses, and physicians all have ethical codes and are to follow these when working with a client in crisis. Modeled after the Hippocratic Oath—"above all, do no harm"—these codes guide professionals as they provide services. Yet, I know of no similar document outlining ethical standards for crisis workers who are volunteers. Although the American Association of Suicidology recommends 40 hours of training, some of which touches on ethics and legal issues for anyone working in crisis intervention (Hoff & Wells, 1989), the question is whether or not this is sufficient. The real question, however, is whether an ethical code, or a set of standards, can guide volunteer crisis workers as they help people in crisis. The obvious response is "yes." Given the potential to manipulate and exploit people in crisis, those who provide services must conduct themselves using a set of principles that protect the client. But which code, which set of standards, should be used, and how should it be applied?

Seeley (1996) believes that a critical factor in understanding and resolving ethical and legal issues concerns supervision—who is supervising the volunteer crisis worker? If

141

volunteers are supervised by licensed human service workers (e.g., psychologists, social workers, professional counselors), they are covered by the license of the supervisor or the facility in which the services are rendered. Therefore, when ethical and legal dilemmas arise, volunteer crisis workers should follow and be protected by the ethical standards of that profession. For example, if a person in crisis discloses some disquieting information regarding the commission of a crime, volunteer crisis workers should follow the ethical standards considered common for that profession. However, if no supervision is being used, professional ethical standards may not apply. In these situations, crisis workers may not be able to claim confidentiality as a reason not to disclose information to authorities.

Another issue concerns liability. To what degree are volunteer crisis workers held liable for providing help to someone in crisis? Most states have what are termed "Good Samaritan laws," which absolve anyone who renders aid gratuitously in an emergency from all liability and negligence. Yet the formulation of these laws varies from state to state (Seeley, 1993). The primary question is whether or not the crisis is an emergency; an example would be someone ready to commit suicide, with the means readily available. But crises are not necessarily emergencies—for example, a person who has experienced the death of a spouse who does not show any sign of suicidal ideation. In these situations, whatever assistance is provided may fall outside the scope of the Good Samaritan law.

A parallel issue concerns malpractice insurance. Unfortunately, lawsuits have become common in the United States; people are sued everyday for everything from meaningful wrongs to trivial incidents that have harmed no one. Consequently, precautions must be taken to ensure that the care given meets the standards set by the community. Taking these precautions means maintaining appropriate records; keeping lines of communication open among professional staff, administration, and volunteers; and keeping all crisis workers informed of changes in ethical guidelines and legal statutes. For example, crisis workers need to understand regulations regarding offering services to minors; confidentiality of information provided by minors; abortion laws, especially with respect to minors; mandated reporting of child or elderly abuse, which may be different for professional human service workers and volunteers; and reporting information about sexually transmitted diseases. Every state will have different laws pertaining to these issues and many more. Crisis workers must keep abreast of these in order to ensure that reasonable care has been provided. The question that inevitably emerges is whether or not volunteer crisis workers are covered by an agency's malpractice insurance and whether that agency is covered in case volunteers are unethical or provide illegal help. Answering that question simply involves contacting the insurance provider and asking, (a) What are the limits to coverage in terms of both money and number and type of incidents? and (b) Who is covered and who is not? While other questions may also be asked, these two are critical in understanding the scope of coverage.

Although ethical and legal issues overlap, it is important to remember that they are different. With respect to ethical guidelines, crisis workers' accountability varies depending on what, if any, professional organization they belong to. If a crisis worker is a member of the American Counseling Association, he or she is subject to that organization's ethical standards. If the crisis worker is a member of the American Psychology Association, he or she is subject to ethical guidelines of that group, and so on. If, on the other hand, a crisis worker is not a member of any professional organization, as is the situation for most volunteers, he or she is not subject to a specific set of ethical guidelines. However, that does not mean the crisis worker has no accountability. Legal issues concern statutes or laws developed by federal, state, or local governments. Regardless of professional affiliation or lack thereof, everyone is responsible for knowing the applicable laws. These laws have been passed by a governmental body and, if breached, a crisis worker may be subject to prosecution. All crisis workers must be aware of and adhere to the legal responsibilities governing the community and geographic location in which they live. I encourage crisis workers to consult with the agency for which they work to determine what ethical standards have been established or are typically observed for working with clients.

A related issue concerns the "duty to warn" if a client is threatening others. Brought to the forefront by the Tarasoff vs. California case (Swenson, 1993), the "duty to warn" is a much debated issue in the professional literature, with only a very general consensus having been reached. Another topic that has received much debate during the past decade is breaking confidentiality when clients disclose they are HIV positive (e.g., Cohen, 1997; Hughes & Friedman, 1994; Lamb, Clark, Drumheller, Frizzell, & Surrey, 1989). Crisis workers must be sensitive to the need to warn others should clients pose a threat—but the procedures for warning others varies depending on what clients disclose and on agency guidelines. If clients disclose a specific threat, crisis workers may be compelled to contact the person to whom the threat was made. General threats made by clients may need to be communicated to local law enforcement. In addition, if crisis workers assess a person as dangerous either to self or others, involuntary commitment procedures should be initiated. Again, during the assessment process, clients may disclose disturbing information. Once this information is disclosed, crisis workers must know how to proceed ethically and legally.

Critical in the assessment process is documentation, especially if clients pose a danger to self or others (Bednar, Bednar, Lambert, & Waite, 1991; Bongar et al., 1998). Crisis workers should document everything they do to ensure clients' safety during the assessment process. Documentation should include the following as appropriate:

1. Questions asked to determine clients' potential for harming themselves or others.
2. Suggestions made to clients that were intended to ensure clients' safety.
3. Interventions initiated to decrease the possibility clients would harm themselves or others.
4. Clinical opinions regarding clients' capacity to determine right from wrong.
5. Clinical opinions regarding clients' stability with respect to not harming themselves or others.
6. Probable diagnosis if appropriate. Also, diagnoses to be ruled out.
7. Clients' statements and agreements not to harm themselves or others.
8. Consultation with other professionals and/or supervisors.

These suggestions are meant to protect crisis workers. Should the worst happen, such as a client committing suicide or homicide, crisis workers and their records are subject to subpoena. If subpoenaed, crisis workers must demonstrate that they have provided the due standard of care. Remember that the practice of informed consent is superseded when clients' safety is jeopardized (Bednar et al., 1991). The protection of clients takes precedence over clients agreeing to treatment in emergency situations. The belief is that if clients were able to consent, they would do so. The issue, though, is what constitutes an emergency. A generally accepted practice involves judging the urgency of the situation, that is, the immediate consequences of foregoing treatment. If crisis workers assess that a client's behavioral reaction to a crisis is potentially harmful to self or others, and if treatment is not administered immediately, they can take whatever steps are necessary to ensure no harm is done, without clients' consent.

A precaution agencies may take to minimize their risk is to set a policy concerning providing services for clients in crisis (Kleespies & Blackburn, 1998). These policies should include setting ethical expectations of anyone providing services by adopting an ethical code developed by a professional organization and informing crisis workers of these expectations. Training standards for providing services may include requirements for updating skills and knowledge of ethical and legal issues; plans to routinely receive consultation or supervision for specific types of crises, such as suicidal or homicidal clients; standards for documentation of services, including case notes and contact charts; and procedures for handling difficult and repeat clients, especially important for agencies sponsoring a hotline. This policy should lead to consistent levels of care and decreased risk in regard to claims of negligence or deviation from what is considered reasonable care.

Likewise, crisis workers can protect themselves from unnecessary risks. The following suggestions are made to help crisis workers, especially those who are volunteers, ensure they are providing services that meet the standard of reasonable care. Crisis workers must know:

1. If they are protected by an ethical code developed by a professional organization. If they are, crisis workers should ask to be informed of that code. If not, I suggest that they encourage the organization to adopt an ethical code on which ethical decisions can be based.

2. That ethics codes are generally more conservative than legal statutes and can be enforced only by professional organizations. By "more conservative," I mean more strict. Crisis workers must understand that ethical codes and legal statutes are not the same and that laws vary from state to state.

3. That there may be times when ethics and the law are in opposition. Confidentiality is an area that often falls into this category. An ethical code may state that client information is to be kept confidential, but the law may say that confidence is to be broken under certain circumstances, such as abuse, threat to harm someone, and threat to commit a felony, to name a few.

4. That all written records are subject to subpoena. Care must be taken when crisis workers are documenting contacts. The judicial system may require that any interview schedule, any standardized test, or the Triage Assessment Form: Crisis Intervention, if used, must be made public in a court of law.

5. The limits of confidentiality for that state. This is especially true when crisis workers are helping minors. Some states prevent the disclosure of information to parents or guardians if this is requested by the minor receiving services. This means that crisis workers are legally prevented from disclosing information to parents or guardians if the minor wants the information to be kept confidential.

6. To consult with someone and document the consultation when in doubt. Consultation should be mandatory in situations involving suicidal or homicidal threats and circumstances in which abuse is suspected.

7. That dual relationships (e.g., sexual relationships with clients, business ventures with clients, and so on) are to be avoided if at all possible. Given the vulnerability of a person in crisis, crisis workers, whether professional or volunteer, should make every effort to sidestep situations in which a dual relationship is present.

8. The laws applying to working with minors, especially when this involves a crisis in which referral for medical treatment may be needed.

Crisis workers must make every effort to practice ethically and within the scope of the law. This type of practice serves to protect clients in crisis and ultimately helps crisis workers provide the best services possible. If volunteer crisis workers have no formal ethical code, they should endeavor to be ethical in the help they offer.

REFERENCES

Bednar, R. L., Bednar, S. C., Lambert, M. J., & Waite, D. R. (1991). *Psychotherapy with high-risk clients: Legal and professional standards.* Pacific Grove, CA: Brooks/Cole.

Bongar, B., Berman, A. L., Maris, R. M., Silverman, M. M., Harris, E. A., & Packman, W. L. (1998). *Risk management with suicidal patients.* New York: Guilford.

Cohen, E. D. (1997). Confidentiality, HIV, and the ACA [American Counseling Association] code of ethics. *Journal of Mental Health Counseling, 19,* 349–363.

Hoff, L. A., & Wells, J. O. (Eds.). (1989). *Certification standards manual* (3rd ed.). Denver: American Association of Suicidology.

Hughes, R. B., & Friedman, A. L. (1994). AIDS-related ethical and legal issues for mental health professionals. *Journal of Mental Health Counseling, 16,* 445–458.

Kleespies, P. M., & Blackburn, E. J. (1998). The emergency telephone call. In P. M. Kleespies (Ed.), *Emergencies in mental health practice: Evaluation and management* (pp. 174–198). New York; Guilford.

Lamb, D. H., Clark, C., Drumheller, P., Frizzell, K., & Surrey, L. (1989). Applying Tarasoff to AIDS-related psychotherapy issues. *Professional Psychology: Research and Practice, 20,* 37–43.

Seeley, M. F. (1993). Hotlines—Legal issues. *Crisis, 14,* 14–15.

Seeley, M. F. (1996). A hotline ethical dilemma. *Crisis, 17,* 53–54.

Swenson, L. C. (1993). *Psychology and law for the helping professions.* Pacific Grove, CA: Brooks/Cole.

Triage Assessment Form: Crisis Intervention*

© R. A. Myer, R. C. Williams, A. J. Ottens, and A. E. Schmidt

CRISIS EVENT:

Identify and describe briefly the crisis situation: _____

_____

_____

AFFECTIVE DOMAIN

Identify and describe briefly the affect that is present. (If more than one affect is experienced, rate with #1 being primary, #2 secondary, #3 tertiary.)

ANGER/HOSTILITY: _____

_____

_____

ANXIETY/FEAR: _____

_____

_____

SADNESS/MELANCHOLY: _____

_____

_____

AFFECTIVE SEVERITY SCALE
Circle the number that most closely corresponds with client's reaction to crisis.

1	2	3	4	5	6	7	8	9	10
No Impairment	**Minimal Impairment**		**Low Impairment**		**Moderate Impairment**		**Marked Impairment**		**Severe Impairment**
Stable mood with normal variation of affect appropriate to daily functioning.	Affect appropriate to situation. Brief periods during which negative mood is experienced slightly more intensely than situation warrants. Emotions are substantially under client control.		Affect appropriate to situation but increasingly longer periods during which negative mood is experienced slightly more intensely than situation warrants. Client perceives emotions as being substantially under control.		Affect may be incongruent with situation. Extended periods of intense negative moods. Mood is experienced noticeably more intensely than situation warrants. Lability of affect may be present. Effort required to control emotions.		Negative affect experienced at markedly higher level than situation warrants. Affects may be obviously incongruent with situation. Mood swings, if occurring, are pronounced. Onset of negative moods are perceived by client as not being under volitional control.		Decompensation or depersonalization evident.

*Used by permission of authors.

COGNITIVE DOMAIN

Identify if a transgression, threat, or loss has occurred in the following areas and describe briefly. (If more than one cognitive response occurs, rate with #1 being primary, #2 secondary, #3 tertiary.)

PHYSICAL (food, water, safety, shelter, etc.):

TRANSGRESSION _____   THREAT _____   LOSS _____

_____

_____

PSYCHOLOGICAL (self-concept, emotional well-being, identity, etc.):

TRANSGRESSION _____   THREAT _____   LOSS _____

_____

_____

SOCIAL RELATIONSHIPS (family, friends, co-workers, etc.):

TRANSGRESSION _____   THREAT _____   LOSS _____

_____

_____

MORAL/SPIRITUAL (personal integrity, values, belief system, etc.):

TRANSGRESSION _____   THREAT _____   LOSS _____

_____

_____

COGNITIVE SEVERITY SCALE

Circle the number that most closely corresponds with client's reaction to crisis.

1	2	3	4	5	6	7	8	9	10
No Impairment	**Minimal Impairment**		**Low Impairment**		**Moderate Impairment**		**Marked Impairment**		**Severe Impairment**
Concentration intact. Client displays normal problem-solving and decision-making abilities. Client's perception and interpretation of crisis event match with reality of situation.	Client's thoughts may drift to crisis event but focus of thoughts is under volitional control. Problem-solving and decision-making abilities minimally affected. Client's perception and interpretation of crisis event substantially match with reality of situation.		Occasional disturbance of concentration. Client perceives diminished control over thoughts of crisis event. Client experiences recurrent difficulties with problem-solving and decision-making abilities. Client's perception and interpretation of crisis event may differ in some respects with reality of situation.		Frequent disturbance of concentration. Intrusive thoughts of crisis event with limited control. Problem-solving and decision-making abilities adversely affected by obsessiveness, self-doubt, confusion. Client's perception and interpretation of crisis event may differ noticeably with reality of situation.		Client plagued by intrusiveness of thoughts regarding crisis event. The appropriateness of client's problem-solving and decision-making abilities likely adversely affected by obsessiveness, self-doubt, confusion. Client's perception and interpretation of crisis event may differ substantially with reality of situation.		Gross inability to concentrate on anything except crisis event. Client so afflicted by obsessiveness, self-doubt, confusion that problem-solving and decision-making abilities have "shut down." Client's perception and interpretation of crisis event may differ so substantially from reality of situation as to constitute threat to client's welfare.

BEHAVIORAL DOMAIN

Identify and describe briefly which behavior is currently being used. (If more than one behavior is utilized, rate with #1 being primary, #2 secondary, #3 tertiary.)

APPROACH: _____

_____

_____

AVOIDANCE: _____

_____

_____

IMMOBILITY: _____

_____

_____

BEHAVIORAL SEVERITY SCALE

Circle the number that most closely corresponds with client's reaction to crisis.

1	2	3	4	5	6	7	8	9	10
No Impairment	**Minimal Impairment**		**Low Impairment**		**Moderate Impairment**		**Marked Impairment**		**Severe Impairment**
Coping behavior appropriate to crisis event. Client performs those tasks necessary for daily functioning.	Occasional utilization of ineffective coping behaviors. Client performs those tasks a necessary for daily functioning, but does so with noticeable effort.		Occasional utilization of ineffective coping behaviors. Client neglects some tasks necessary for daily functioning is noticeably compromised.		Client displays coping behaviors that are likely to exacerbate crisis situation. Ability to perform tasks necessary for daily functioning is noticeably compromised.		Client displays coping behaviors that are likely to exacerbate crisis situation. Ability to perform tasks necessary for daily functioning is markedly absent.		Behavior is erratic, unpredictable. Client's behaviors are harmful to self and/or others.

DOMAIN SEVERITY SCALE SUMMARY

Affective _____
Cognitive _____
Behavioral _____
Total _____

Index

Ability to function, 91–92, 94–96, 103
Active behaviors, 89, 100, 121
Adaptive coping behavior, 100–101
Advice giving, 110
Affect versus mood, 42
Affective intervention strategies, 116–18
Affective reactions assessment: affect versus mood, 42; approach to, 41–46; and client's pain shared by crisis workers, 38–39; client's self-report, 41–42; commonly used affective words, 45–46; and connection to intervention, 116–18; and crisis workers' emotional reaction to client, 39; crisis workers' role in, 37–39; description of affective reactions, 39–41; duration of affective reaction, 51; expression of emotions by client, 37–38; first impressions of affective reactions, 47–48; guidelines for, 46; inflated rating, 52; intensity of feelings or moods, 51–52; nonverbal indicators of severity, 42–44, 47–48; observation for severity, 47–49; precautions concerning, 52; primary emotions and crises, 39–41; questions for, 44–46; report of others, 49; severity assessment, 46–52; severity rating assignment, 49–52; summary and points to remember, 52–53; too-low rating, 52; in triage assessment model, 29–30; verbal indicators of severity, 42–44, 48–49; vignette on, 36–37; voice qual-

ity, 44, 48–49. *See also* Triage Assessment Form (TAF)
Affective Severity Scale, 49–52, 115–16, 147
African Americans, 87
Aguilera, D. C., 89
Akiskal, H. S., 73
Akiskal, K., 73
American Counseling Association, 142
American Psychology Association, 142
Anger/hostility: commonly used affective words, 45; expression of, 42; guidelines for assessment of, 46; as primary emotion, 40; as response to crisis, 41; in triage assessment model, 29–30; and voice quality, 44
Anxiety. *See* Fear/anxiety
Approach behaviors, as reaction to crisis, 90, 92, 94–95
Asian Americans and Asian refugees, 68, 87
Assessment. *See* Crisis assessment
Avoidance behaviors, as reaction to crisis, 90, 92, 94–96
Awareness strategy, 117–18

Baldwin, B. A., 23–24
Bancroft, 90
BASIC-ID assessment, 26
BDI. *See* Beck Depression Inventory (BDI)
Beck Depression Inventory (BDI), 12
Beck Scale for Suicidal Ideation, 21
Behavioral intervention strategies, 119–20